Basic Statistics

Basic Statistics
for medical and social science students

A. E. MAXWELL

Past Professor of Psychological Statistics,
Institute of Psychiatry, University of London

LONDON NEW YORK

CHAPMAN AND HALL

First published in 1972 by
Penguin Books Ltd as
Basic Statistics in Behavioural Research
This Science Paperback edition
first published 1978 by Chapman and Hall,
11 New Fetter Lane, London EC4P 4EE
Reprinted 1983

© A. E. Maxwell

Printed in Great Britain by
J. W. Arrowsmith Ltd, Bristol

Contents

Preface

For many years now I have been required to give a series of elementary lectures on statistics to medical students about to undertake a postgraduate course in psychiatry. The declared aim of the course, for which very limited time was available, was to provide the students with some initial understanding of the statistical terminology and elementary techniques to which other teachers, in particular psychologists and sociologists, would be likely to refer in the course of their lectures. The task was tricky for two reasons. In the first place most of the students involved, despite their best intentions, had forgotten their school mathematics, and secondly no textbook existed at the right level of difficulty which contained examples appropriate to these students' needs and experience.

The present book was written to fill the gap. Though primarily intended for psychiatrists, the book should prove very useful to any student of the behavioural sciences who wants a simple introductory course on the principles of experimental design and data analysis. It must be one of the simplest textbooks on elementary statistics ever written.

I am indebted to the literary executor of the late Sir Ronald A. Fisher, F.R.S., to Dr Frank Yates, F.R.S., and to Oliver & Boyd Ltd for permission to reprint Tables 3 and 5 from their book *Statistical Tables for Biological, Agricultural and Medical Research*.

I am also indebted to Professor E. S. Pearson on behalf of the B ometrika trustees, for permission to reproduce in abridged form Table 8 frcm E. S. Pearson and H. O. Hartley, *Biometrika Tables for Statisticians* Volume 1, Cambridge University Press, 1954.

Finally I would like to thank Professor W. M. O'Neil for several suggestions aimed at clarifying the text and Miss Nina Aitken who typed the manuscript with consummate care.

Basic Statistics

1 Some Common Types of Investigation

Introduction

When the history of science in the first half of the twentieth century comes to be written there is no doubt that *Statistics* will occupy a very important chapter. This new discipline has been developed largely in the last fifty years and already has come to play a leading role in most branches of scientific research whether they are concerned with well-controlled laboratory experiments or with large, less precise and less well-defined observational surveys in the field. Indeed, if we confine our attention to research in the behavioural and medical sciences, with which this book is concerned, it is hard to imagine investigations being satisfactorily carried on today without the aid of statistical procedures and methodology. The main reasons are threefold: in the first place the measurements which it is possible to make of variables such as reaction times, muscle tension, learning speeds, intelligence, not to mention anxiety, depression, thought disorder, and so forth, are so variable – not only from person to person but also for a single person at different times – that it would be difficult to describe our findings without the aid of summary statistical measures. In the second place it is generally impracticable to record data for all members of the class of individuals in which we are interested in any particular investigation and we have to be content with a sample from it. Here again statistical theory is essential in telling us how best to draw our sample and in assisting us to make inferences about the complete class on the basis of data derived from a sample only. Finally, it is the case that much of the information derived from experiments and investigations comes from making comparisons between deliberately chosen, or perhaps just recognizable, sub-groups of people or things, so that once more we must turn to statistical theory to discover how the comparisons may reliably be made.

It appears then that some knowledge of statistics is desirable for the successful conduct of research in the behavioural sciences. Now statistics, on the theoretical side, is a branch of mathematics, so that a full understanding of its basic principles lies beyond the attainments of most behavioural scientists. Fortunately the application of a considerable part of elementary statistical methodology – if the basic theory is taken for granted – is relatively straightforward and can, with care, be used by the amateur. At any rate he will find himself better equipped to communicate with a statistician if he already has some knowledge of statistical terminology and reasoning. The aim of this introductory course is to supply him with this information.

Types of Investigation

It may be helpful at the outset to try and classify some of the more common types of investigations carried out in the behavioural sciences and then to indicate the relevance of statistical methods to each.

Many investigations are primarily fact-finding in nature. For instance, one recent study consisted of a stocktaking of the whereabouts and present posts of psychiatrists trained at the Institute of Psychiatry and Maudsley–Bethlem Hospitals. The study was confined to junior grades of staff up to and including senior registrars trained in the period 1946 to 1958, and who since then had left to work elsewhere. The first count made was one of 'country of origin' of the individuals concerned: this yielded the following figures:

Country of origin

U.K.	Abroad	Total
186	88	274

These figures were then subdivided into 'country of present post'.

		Country of origin	
		U.K.	*Abroad*
Present	*U.K.*	153	22
post	*Abroad*	33	66

The study continued by seeking reasons why psychiatrists born in the U.K. went abroad and why those born abroad and trained in the U.K. had decided to remain here. It also investigated, amongst other things, the types of post which psychiatrists in each category now held and the trends which had occurred over the years as they moved from one type of post (teaching, research, clinical, etc.) to another.

This is a relatively straightforward fact-finding type of study and involves a minimum amount of statistical methodology. The information sought is obtained in part at least by a successive breakdown of categories into sub-categories, and it is obvious that a fairly large sample of individuals is required in the first instance if the process of breakdown is to be taken beyond two or three steps, for otherwise the numbers in each sub-class soon become too small to yield reliable information. But though the study involves little statistics as such, it is beset by difficulties of a different sort. These are often difficulties of definition. For instance the term 'present post' may be tricky to define because a psychiatrist may divide his time amongst several different types of post. Also, the drawing up of a questionnaire designed to obtain by mail the information necessary for the inquiry requires special attention. In this respect the advice of a statistician is generally desirable if the questions are to be cast in a form which will allow the information to be transferred on to punch cards for easy mechanical sorting or analysis on a computer (see chapter 10).

Hypothesis testing in observational studies

In contrast to the fact-finding type of study just described, some observational studies are carried out to test a particular hypothesis which the investigator has in mind. A good example is a study done some years ago in the Baltimore district of the U.S.A. One of the hypotheses to be tested was that cerebral damage in the foetus and at birth was a contributing factor to development of abnormal behaviour patterns in the child. The main problem here was that of finding, in the population of children, samples on which the hypothesis could be tested with some exactitude. What was required on the one hand was a sample of children with known abnormal behaviour patterns for whom reliable hospital records concerning complications of pregnancy and labour, length of gestation and possible operative procedures at delivery, were available. On the other hand a control group was needed for comparative purposes. This group had to consist of children comparable to the first group as regards age, socio-economic status, home background and educational environment, etc., and differing only from the former in so far as they were not abnormal with regard to behaviour. They too had to have been born in hospital so that reliable records of pregnancy and delivery would be available.

It is easy to appreciate that the task of securing two relatively large groups of children meeting the requirements of the investigation was not easy. In the Baltimore study an initial sample of 1800 children with general behaviour disorders was reduced by about 75 per cent as a result of the selection necessary to secure a group meeting the requirements of the investigation, and this latter group had to be further subdivided since it included 'whites' and 'non-whites'.

Frequently, of course, groups which we may wish to compare with respect to some attribute or variable are readily found in nature. Many examples could be cited: we might for instance be interested in comparing the verbal attainments of boys and girls of a given age, or the reading habits of children with television sets in their homes and those with no television sets. Or we might wish to compare the incidence of hallucinations, obsessional fears, or other psychiatric variables, in patients from different diagnostic categories; and so on. Useful information is often obtained when groups such as these are compared provided every effort is made to equate the groups on other variables which might bias the comparison. Generalization of the results obtained will depend on how representative the samples in the comparison are of the classes of individuals being compared.

Experience has shown that the process of trying to obtain two groups which are alike in all respects save only in the factors or attributes on which they are to be compared is difficult – though perfect matching will not be essential if the differences being investigated are substantial. Indeed, if matching of groups is carried too far there is sometimes a danger that we may inadvertently achieve a partial matching on the very factors we wish to compare. For example, if the aim of an investigation is to compare the verbal attainment of boys and girls of similar age, it would be dangerous to match them on I.Q., since verbal attainment and scores on a test of general intelligence tend to be highly correlated. In such a case it would be advisable to base the comparison on fairly large samples of boys and girls drawn randomly from the population, or to take into account only major disrupting factors such as known differences between rural and urban groups and between children from differing socio-economic backgrounds.

Retrospective and prospective studies

The Baltimore study just referred to is typical of what is generally described as a *retrospective* study. It began with a plausible cause-and-effect hypothesis and an investigation was carried out backwards in time to see if the suspected cause was indeed associated with the postulated effect. This type of study, though clearly cumbersome, has the advantage that patients already known to have an illness can readily be identified and the problem of investigating the cause can be tackled without undue delay.

By contrast, studies of the type which proceed forward in time are known as *prospective*. In such cases note is made of the occurrence of an event which is thought to have possible harmful consequences and the subject is kept under observation to see if these materialize. An often quoted example is that of the association between rubella during pregnancy and congenital cataract in the child. The association was first noted in 1941 by Gregg in Australia and the question arose of estimating the extent of the risk. Retrospective studies were first undertaken by asking mothers of defective children if they had had rubella during their pregnancy. But this method proved unsatisfactory for a number of reasons. Rubella is a relatively mild disease so that mothers' reports about having it were often unreliable. In addition, mothers who had had rubella and whose children escaped the disease often went undetected. To obtain reliable information it was necessary to carry out prospective studies by following up women who during pregnancy contracted rubella: the incidence of congenital cataract in the children was then noted.

Prospective studies have obvious advantages over retrospective ones in so far as there is less opportunity for bias in the results, but they are often difficult to organize and may be slow and expensive if the disease in question is rare.

The probability of events

An important point to note about cause-and-effect relationships is that the cause of an illness, even if it is undisputed, is not necessarily followed in every instance by the associated effect. This is so because of the very complicated set of circumstances and interactions, such as the present state of health of an individual or the strength of his immunity to a particular infection, which may be called into play during the incubation period of a disease. As a consequence, considerable variability between the reactions of different individuals to infection may be expected. In brief, one finds that one is dealing with *probabilities* rather than with *certainties*. To illustrate the point let us take an example. For many years now it has been universally accepted that the tubercle bacillus is the cause of tuberculosis; yet it does not follow that everyone who is subjected to infection will contract the disease. For instance in Lubeck in Germany in 1926, by an unfortunate accident, 246 babies were inoculated with live tubercular vaccine but happily only seventy-six of the babies died. This fact is illustrative of the intrinsic variability of human reactions and of the type of evidence on which true cause-and-effect relationships may first be detected. Evaluation of such evidence invariably requires the use of statistical procedures.

Summary

A brief outline has now been given of a few of the types of *non-experimental* studies which are constantly being carried out. Their successful conduct clearly requires the investigator to be well informed about the subject-matter of the inquiry and thoroughly familiar with earlier research work and research methods in the field. He must be aware of potential sources of bias and may often have to make decisions about the extent of bias which can be tolerated in cases where it cannot be completely controlled. Because of this need of involvement in subject-matter, statisticians in the past have not contributed greatly to the planning of non-experimental studies, but the principles of design which they have developed in the field of controlled experimentation, to which we now turn, can often be followed with advantage in studies of the former kind.

Controlled Experimentation

As we have seen, one of the main difficulties met in non-experimental studies in interpreting the results of comparisons involving several groups arises from the fact that one cannot always be certain that these groups are alike in all respects save only in the attribute under examination, with the result that an unambiguous interpretation of the outcome of an investigation may prove difficult. One of the most worthwhile contributions made by statisticians to scientific inquiry is directed towards the elimination of ambiguity in the interpretation of results by designing, whenever possible, experiments or investigations in such a way that ambiguity will be less likely to arise. This procedure is possible in many cases of deliberate experimentation; that is, in cases where treatments to be given or tests to be administered are under the experimenter's control, and where the subjects to be tested can be randomly allocated to one group or another (with prior one-to-one matching if desirable or possible). To illustrate the procedure, it may prove informative to consider an early experiment which, though it ended in confusion, would have proved satisfactory had certain essential principles been followed. It is known as the Lanarkshire experiment.

In 1930 it was decided to carry out an experiment in Lanarkshire schools to assess the possible beneficial effects of giving the children free milk during the school day. Twenty thousand children took part and for five months, February to June, half of them had three-quarters of a pint of either raw or pasteurized milk while the remainder did not have milk. All the children were weighed and had their heights measured before and after the experiment, but contrary to expectation the average increase for the children who had not had milk exceeded that for the children who had had milk. This unexpected result was later attributed to unconscious bias in the formation of the groups being compared. In each school the division of the children into a 'milk' or a 'no-milk' group was made either by ballot or by using an alphabetic system, but if the outcome appeared to give groups with an undue preponderance of well-nourished or ill-nourished children some arbitrary interchange was carried out in an effort to balance them. In this interchange the teachers must unconsciously have tended to put a preponderance of ill-nourished children into the group receiving milk. The results of the experiment were further complicated by the fact that the children were weighed in their clothes and this probably introduced a differential effect as between winter and summer and children from poorer and wealthier homes. Because of the deficiencies in design the results of the experiment were ambiguous despite the very large sample of children concerned.

A statistician designing such an experiment today would insist on strict random allocation of subjects to groups – a point to which we shall shortly return, as it is one of the keys to good experimental design. Of course, if there were good ethical reasons why certain children should have milk at any cost, then these children must have it, but matters would have to be arranged so that they could later be omitted from the comparison. Ethical problems do arise where experiments with human subjects are concerned and these are often difficult to circumvent without damage to the project in hand. An interesting case occurred in an investigation some years ago concerned with the treatment of *polyarteritis nodosa* with *cortisone*. This new treatment was thought to hold great prospects as compared with standard treatments and the doctors involved in the investigation felt that no patient could reasonably be denied it. As a consequence it was decided to compare the results of treating patients with cortisone with those obtained in the same hospitals, using other treatments, during the previous ten years. The latter were to provide the controls. But when the comparison between the two groups of patients came to be made, it was found that the control group contained more patients with *hypertension* than did the experimental group, and as hypertension is an important factor in prognosis where this disease is concerned, no valid conclusions could be drawn. The answer to the ethical dilemma may be that we should not be too influenced by unproved claims for new treatments and new methods until they are well established.

Randomization in controlled investigations

The two experiments just considered lead us to the first requirement in the conduct of a comparative investigation: before the experiment begins and the different treatments or tests to be compared are administered, we must ensure that we have groups which are equivalent in all respects apart from the treatments which they are to receive. But how are the equivalent groups to be formed?

The statistician's answer to this problem is that the subjects available for the experiment must be allotted to the groups in a truly random way – say by the toss of an unbiased coin or by the use of a table of random numbers. If only two treatments or tests are to be compared, only two groups will be required; the treatments or tests will then be allotted in a random way to the groups and during the conduct of the experiment the environmental conditions of the groups must be kept similar. If different types of subjects are to be included in the experiment, then greater control of extraneous variation is achieved if the randomization is done in a stratified way: for instance, it might be advantageous to randomize males and females separately, or to randomize subjects from different socio-economic groups separately, and so on. This act of objective randomization is the experimenter's safeguard against a biased comparison, and his justification for assuming that errors are random. It is also his guarantee that unambiguous conclusions can be drawn from the results of his experiment. Of course, randomization cannot ensure that the groups are identical in all respects, but it does eliminate the possibility of conscious or unconscious bias in allocation of the kind noted in the Lanarkshire experiment. Moreover, when the allocation is made in a random way, it enables one to calculate the probability – at least within certain known limits of error – that any observed discrepancy between the groups could have arisen by chance.

Subjects as their own controls

The process just described of obtaining groups that are comparable (before treatments are administered) by random or by stratified random allocation of subjects to groups is generally satisfactory when the subjects for inclusion in an experiment are known in advance and their number is not too small so that possible initial differences between groups cancel each other out. In other cases, and especially when variability between subjects is considerable, greater precision can be achieved if the experiment is designed so that each subject has each treatment. With the latter procedure comparison between treatments is made 'within subjects', and large differences 'between subjects', which would tend to blur the outcome, are eliminated. But this type of design may present difficulties of its own, especially if the conditions or states of the subjects change during the course of the experiment. Such changes can be allowed for, if they are linear in nature, by balancing the order in which the treatments are administered. The simplest case is that in which two treatments, say A and B (one of which might be a placebo), are to be compared. If the sample of subjects to be included in the experiment is known in advance, then it can be randomly divided into two equal sub-samples, one of which has treatment A in the first treatment session and B in the second, while the second sub-sample has the treatments in the reverse order. In this way order effects in the data can be eliminated and an unbiased comparison of the treatments obtained. But it is unwise to rely too heavily on simple rules. For instance it may happen that a subject, say a psychiatric patient, has to be kept on a treatment for a number of weeks before its effect has time to show. By this time the patient may either have recovered, or changed so radically that switching him onto a second treatment would either be unwarranted or would be meaningless as regards a comparison of the two treatments. If such an eventuality were likely, then a design in which a patient was to have different treatments in succession would be unsuitable.

Other fairly obvious precautions also have to be taken in experiments with human subjects and in situations in which truly objective recording of the results is impossible. Good examples are the so-called 'blind' and 'double-blind' trials carried out in the relative assessment of different drugs. In 'blind' trials the patients are kept in ignorance of the particular drug being administered at any stage of the experiment. This is especially desirable if the experimenter has to rely on self-ratings by the patients. In 'double-blind' trials both the patients and the doctor or nurse assessing the treatment effects are, in as far as is possible, kept unaware of the particular treatments they are trying to assess.

The comparison of several treatments
When several treatments, or several levels of the same treatment, are to be compared, and it is inconvenient or impossible because of scarcity of subjects to have a separate group for each, more elaborate designs can occasionally be employed. A fairly common one is the Latin-square design and an experiment in which such a design was used will now be briefly described. It was concerned with the relative merits of three different barbiturate preparations, each at two levels, on the production of sleep in human subjects. A placebo 'treatment' was also included (on two occasions) so that there were eight treatments in all. They were administered to hospital patients at bedtime in the form of tablets which were alike in shape, colour and taste so that the patients were unaware that different treatments were involved. The statistical problem was one of

designing an experiment which would make possible an unbiased comparison of the effectiveness of the treatments for inducing and maintaining sleep.

One way of doing this experiment would be to try out each treatment on a separate group of patients and then to compare the results obtained. But the possibility of being able to set up as many as eight comparable groups simultaneously and of ensuring that (apart from the treatments) their environment and nursing were similar during the experiment, would be remote. Moreover, since one of the treatments is a placebo, introduced for control purposes, an ethical problem might arise if it were proposed to keep a particular group of patients on it for any considerable length of time. To circumvent these difficulties a Latin-square design was employed.

A Latin square is a square array of letters in which any given letter occurs once in each row and once in each column of the array. Examples of Latin squares and instructions on how to choose one of a given size at random from the numerous possibilities will be found in Fisher and Yates's book, *Statistical Tables* (1963). An example of an 8×8 square is given below: this size of square is relevant in the present discussion since we wish to compare eight treatments.

An 8 × 8 Latin square

D	C	A	G	H	F	B	E
B	E	H	F	G	A	D	C
F	G	E	H	C	D	A	B
E	H	G	B	D	C	F	A
C	A	B	D	E	G	H	F
A	B	C	E	F	H	G	D
G	D	F	C	A	B	E	H
H	F	D	A	B	E	C	G

If each of the eight letters, A to H, is now assigned – preferably at random – to one of the eight treatments, then we can refer to a treatment by the letter which denotes it. Now if the successive columns of the square are taken to refer to eight consecutive nights, and eight patients for inclusion in the experiment are allotted at random to the eight rows of the square, we have a balanced design in which each patient on each consecutive night gets a different treatment. Moreover, for every batch of eight patients each treatment is administered an equal number of times.

This arrangement has certain obvious advantages – and certain, less obvious, disadvantages. One advantage is that the placebo, which has been included in the design to provide control data, is administered only twice to each patient and this resolves the ethical problem. Another advantage is that since each treatment is administered once on the first night of the experiment, once on the second night, and so on, no single treatment can on the average be deemed to have an advantage over another should it be the case that the patients' conditions were gradually improving as the experiment proceeded. Of course, should it so happen that the patients' conditions were changing in a differential way, then a certain amount of bias in the subsequent comparisons of the treatments would probably be present; to some extent this can be guarded against by the choice of patients to be included in the experiment in the first instance. There is the possibility too that different patients might react differently to different treatments, but this is unlikely with drugs bearing a strong family resemblance. Disrupting effects of the kind just mentioned have to be borne in mind, but if they may be considered to be relatively unimportant the design has many advantages. One is mathematical for it so happens that when the experiment is conducted in the manner indicated three independent sets of comparisons can readily be made. One is the comparison of the treatments themselves; another is the comparison of patients' average progress on the successive nights; while a third is a comparison between the individual patients, which will give an indication of how much individual variation to expect. A final aspect of the experiment refers to the measurements to be taken and to the actual calculations necessary in making the comparisons, but these problems will be deferred for the present.

Some basic principles
A Latin-square design is only one example of the numerous types of experimental design which statisticians have invented.

While it would be impossible to describe even a selection of them here, a few principles basic to the planning of experiments are worth emphasizing. The importance of randomization in the construction of comparable groups has already been stressed. Another basic notion is that of replication. In a comparative investigation little confidence can be placed in results obtained with just a few cases because of the inherent variability in subjects' reactions and responses in test situations, and because of the difficulty of obtaining relatively reliable measures of response. If variability is great, precision can in general only be achieved by the use of fairly large samples. How large can only be decided in advance if some prior knowledge of the variability to be expected is available.

A further basic principle in good experimentation is concerned with local control of variability. For example, in a drug trial, if it is known or suspected that fat patients are likely to react less to a given dosage of a drug than lean patients, then random allocation of subjects to groups should be carried out separately for these two types, or at least the weights of the patients should be noted so that adjustments can be made when the results are being analysed.

Finally, it is helpful to realize that many of the principles applied in controlled experiments can frequently be employed to great advantage in the design of non-experimental studies. An example will help to illustrate what is implied. The study was concerned with the role played by age and sex in children's absence from school due to a number of causes, one of which was 'infection of the respiratory tract'. Eight randomly selected samples of thirty children each, four of boys and four of girls of ages six, seven, eight and nine years respectively, were drawn from the records of children attending three London schools. The children were followed up for three consecutive years and the average number of absences for each year for each child was found. The systematic way in which the study was planned meant that the data could be analysed readily and efficiently according to a well-known classic design (a split-plot design). Note in particular that the samples were randomly drawn to eliminate bias and that perfect balance was maintained between the sexes as regards the numbers in the samples, the age range covered and the period of follow-up. Had the eight samples, for instance, been unequal in size, or the age range or period of follow-up been different from one sample to another, an adequate analysis of the data would have proved very complicated indeed, even for a professional statistician.

2 Measurement

The essence of objective investigation and scientific experimentation is measurement. In observational field studies the measurements are frequently straightforward counts; for example, the number of school days in a year that a child is absent due to colds, or the number of people in a given district who are in need of psychiatric treatment. In such instances the problem of obtaining reliable information is concerned not so much with measurement *per se* as with general questions such as the definition of terms (e.g. 'colds'), or the possibility of being able to identify and list the people in whom one is interested and, if they are too numerous, in the possibility of drawing an unbiased sample from them.

But in other studies, and in particular in experimental work, we may be interested in continuous variables on each of which a measurement for each member of a sample is required. Here the problem is straightforward if yardsticks for the variables in question are already available. Recently, for instance, a survey was carried out of the heights, weights and intelligence of a cross-section of children attending ordinary day schools in London. Now standard scales exist for measuring such quantities as *height* and *weight*, so these variables presented no difficulty. For intelligence the problem was slightly more complicated. Many tests for measuring 'intelligence' or 'attainment' exist today, but the selection of one that is suitable to any particular situation presents a number of problems. For one thing the choice may depend on the age of the subjects. In the case of children, whose intelligence and attainments increase noticeably as they grow older, the tests chosen must have been constructed and standardized for the age range in question, or they must make allowance for differences in age. In addition, different tests are not necessarily interchangeable and often yield quite conflicting results. This can arise not just because the tests may be of different lengths and so have different maximum scores, but because scores are often expressed as intelligence quotients and the populations on which the different tests were standardized may not have been comparable.

Where adult subjects are concerned, age is generally not so important. But here again results obtained from different tests are seldom interchangeable. For example, in a recent study of feeble-minded patients in the age range sixteen to sixty-six years, the mean I.Q. obtained for a sample of 190 patients using two well-known tests differed considerably:

Test	Mean I.Q.
Stanford–Binet	63·48
Wechsler–Bellevue	80·01

Precision of Measurement

Many of the measurements obtained in laboratory experiments are derived by means of sophisticated electric and electronic apparatus, by the use of highly developed and well-calibrated standard equipment, and so on. But unlike the 'pure' scientist, working in fields in which technology is well advanced, the behavioural scientist is as yet ill equipped. Indeed, behavioural scientists often bemoan their lot since reliable yardsticks do not exist for measuring many of the variables – sensations, attitudes, beliefs, etc. – in which they are interested. Nevertheless, all yardsticks, however simple or however complicated, have to be constructed: they do not exist in nature. Even when constructed they often appear strange at first sight; the fact that temperature is measured by noting the height of a column of mercury in a glass tube could hardly be looked on as a very obvious procedure, yet it does work and we have now grown accustomed to the idea even if on reflection it looks far-fetched.

Yet it cannot be gainsaid that psychological and social variables do present special difficulties as regards measurement. For one thing they are often difficult to define – *anxiety*, *extraversion, originality* are good examples – and even if they can be defined fairly precisely, seldom can they be measured directly. But an effort has to be made and tests of intelligence, for instance, illustrate very well the kinds of instruments which can be constructed to measure mental behaviour.

One essential is that the measurement process undertaken be as objective as possible so that other competent scientists can repeat the process with some hope of confirming results already obtained. For instance, in the days before standardized cognitive tests were introduced it was common practice for medical practitioners to be guided in their decisions about a patient's mental ability or educational achievements by asking him to name the capitals of certain countries or to give the distance from London to Paris, or elsewhere; and so on. The information obtained in this way, needless to say, was unreliable and inadequate for the purpose for which it was intended.

Constructing a Test of Cognitive Ability

Since the construction of objective tests of cognitive ability began over half a century ago a vast amount of literature on the subject has been published. It is well summarized in a recent book by Lord and Novick (1968), which will give the mathematically-minded reader some idea of the intricate technology which specialists in test-construction now have at their command. On the less technical side there are a few basic principles which the amateur can use as a guide and these are summarized below.

Suppose that it is required to construct a test of some aspect of human ability, say a test of 'verbal comprehension' for use with an adult population. The first step would be to assemble a large number of items for possible inclusion in the test. Here are two examples from such a test:

A. From the list of five incomplete words given below
(1) – – ight, (2) – – lume, (3) – – ea, (4) – – stance, (5) – – ltage, write in the brackets the *number* of the word which would complete the following sentence:
'The — to be measured is six miles.'   (   )

B. Amongst the following list of words one word differs in an out-
standing way from the others. Write its number in the brackets.
(1) lyric, (2) elegy, (3) lay, (4) sonata, (5) ballad. (   )

A few preliminary points should now be noted. The purpose of
putting the answer in brackets at the right-hand side of the page
is to facilitate the tedious task of scoring the test and of transferring the data to punch cards for tabulation and analysis. It
is also customary to print beside each set of brackets the number
of the column of the punch card on which the answer is to be
recorded (see chapter 10). Note also that the answer to each
question has to be chosen from a number of alternatives: this
is to reduce the possibility of the subject getting the item correct
by guessing and for this purpose about five to seven alternatives
are desirable.

Having assembled the items it will be necessary to try them
out on a sample of people from the population for which the
test is intended. It is important that this sample is not confined
to people who are readily available or to people you happen to
know, for they might not be representative of the population.
To get a truly representative sample is not an easy matter.
Several possibilities might be feasible. If the population concerned were relatively small and well defined, such as all people
over the age of twenty-one in the Isle of Man or in some new
town or on a housing estate, it might be possible to list and
number the people and then to draw a sample from the numbers
by lottery procedures. This is known as a simple random
sample.

But if the population from which you want to sample is large,
say a city or large rural area, the method of sampling just
described would be too cumbersome and time consuming. It
might now be necessary first to take a random sample of units
bigger than individual people, such as parishes, polling districts
or wards, and thereafter to choose a random sample of people
from each of these larger units. Moreover, if the larger units
themselves can be stratified in such a way that units which
resemble each other are grouped in the same stratum, it will be
beneficial to sample separately from the different strata.

Frequently it will be the case that the individuals in the larger units are already listed, say on the latest register of voters. If this is the case, and if the list is up to date, one might decide on a suitable sampling fraction, say 1 in 20, or 1 in 50, etc., depending on the lengths of the lists and the resources available for the study, and arrive at one's sample in this way. More particularly, if the sampling fraction were 1 in 20, one would first select a number between 1 and 20 at random. If this number were found to be 9 then the individuals chosen from the list would be 9, 29, 49, etc. Since it is unlikely that the names on the list are in random order, this method will not give a *simple random sample*, but experience has shown that it is a fairly satisfactory way to proceed. Several textbooks which give information about how to draw samples when the population is large and heterogeneous are now available; one of the least technical of these is by C. A. Moser (1958).

Having chosen a sample of people and having obtained their answers to the initial list of items, the next important step is to examine the answers to see if the wording of any of the items has proved to be ambiguous, or whether there is more than one acceptable answer to each. As a result of this initial screening a percentage of the items may have to be dropped. The next step is to carry out some form of item analysis to determine which items are good at discriminating between people as regards their verbal comprehension. A good measure of the discriminative power of an item is the variance of the answers given to it by the members of the sample. Normally an item is scored 1 for a correct answer and 0 for an incorrect answer. If the sample size is represented by N and if n members of the sample get an item correct, then the proportion, p, of the sample that gets that item correct is

$$p = \frac{n}{N}. \tag{2.1}$$

The variance (see chapter 3) of the item is then given by

$$\text{var} = pq, \tag{2.2}$$

where $q = 1 - p$. It is easy to show that the variance has its maximum value when $p = q$, that is when 50 per cent of the sample get the item correct. For values of p other than $0 \cdot 5$ but within the range $0 \cdot 2$ and $0 \cdot 8$ the variance is still relatively large, but it tends to decrease sharply for values of p outside this range. This fact should be noted, for at first sight it might appear that only difficult items should be included in the test if it is to differentiate the weak from the strong. That this is not so can be seen by considering extreme cases; for example, items which all members of the sample get correct or incorrect tell us nothing about the relative abilities of the individuals being tested. In constructing a test it is, however, advisable to place a few relatively easy items at the beginning to get the testees off to a good start.

Another and complementary way of ensuring that a test will give good discrimination is to include in it items which correlate highly with each other. Without going to the labour of actually correlating the items, this will be achieved if the items are of medium difficulty and are also reasonably homogeneous as regards content. On the other hand if a computer is available the correlations between the items can be obtained; and if a factor analysis is then carried out, the amount of variance extracted by the first factor will give a good indication of the homogeneity of the set of items taken as a whole. Naturally, if the items are not homogeneous as regards content, two or more factors may prove necessary to account for the intercorrelations; it might then be necessary to subdivide the items and make more than one test. Alternatively, one might exclude from the test items which had relatively small loadings on the first factor and in this way achieve greater homogeneity of content amongst the items retained.

Once the final set of items for inclusion in the test has been decided, the scores (on the test as a whole) obtained by the members of the sample can be calculated. A summary description of the results can then be carried out (see chapter 3) and retained for further use.

Constructing a Simple Rating Scale

Frequently, of course, an experimenter will be faced with problems of measurement less ambitious than that described in the last section. For instance he may wish to construct an *ad hoc*, but objective, measuring instrument for use in some specific investigation. To take an example, let us suppose that he wishes to carry out a trial to assess the relative effects of some tranquillizing drugs for the relief of anxiety in patients.

The first problem in this instance is to get a clear idea of what the term 'anxiety' comprises. While a fully adequate definition of the term might be difficult to formulate, it should still be possible to list the symptoms indicative of the complaint. The list once compiled could then be discussed with other informed people with a view to reaching a fair measure of agreement about the adequacy and relevance of the items included. The outcome would be a catalogue of symptoms, such as: inability to relax; nightmares; panic attacks; tendency to sweat; palpitation; fear of crowds.

Now each of these symptoms might be expected to be present to a greater or lesser degree in different patients and provision would have to be made to allow for differences when recording the results. This could be achieved by employing a rating scale. The scale need not be complex and generally a five-point scale for each item, scored somewhat as follows, is adequate:

Scale gradation	*Score*
Symptom absent	0
Symptom mild	1
Symptom moderate	2
Symptom severe	3
Symptom very severe	4

Such a scale would enable the investigators to score each patient on each symptom and so to quantify the observations in an objective way. The extent to which one rater would get results similar to another, for the same patient, would still of course not be ensured. Agreement would depend on a number of factors. The raters would have to be clear as to what exactly was meant by each symptom and to achieve such agreement some indoctrination of raters would probably be necessary. But even if two raters were in agreement about 'meaning', their results might still disagree were it the case that they were interpreting the levels on the scale differently. Fortunately, the latter type of disagreement is not as serious as the former for bias between raters can easily be checked in the analysis of the final scores and adjustments made if necessary.

The essential requirement is to have a list of well-defined observations to be made and a clear-cut method of scoring. Without these, a fair replication of an investigation will be difficult and agreement between replications poor. Certain valid short cuts in the scoring system may be possible. For example, if the list of symptoms were very long, so that the amount of data collected for each patient tended to be cumbersome, the symptoms might be grouped into categories and a score recorded for each category only. Possible categories in our example might be as follows:

Psychological symptoms including such items as 'fear',
'state of apprehension',
'inability to relax', etc.,
and

Somatic symptoms including such items as
'tendency to sweat',
'palpitation', etc.

By grouping the items in a manner such as this the results could be condensed into a more manageable form.

Complementary Measurements

Frequently in an experiment it is possible to obtain several different types of measurements or ratings which may supply complementary pieces of information. For instance in the Latin-square design described in chapter 1, one measure of the effects of the soporific drugs was a relatively objective one, as the beds which the patients occupied were fitted with a mechanical device which gave a continuous record of their movement during the night. Additional information was obtained by the nurses, who kept a record of the total amount of time each patient slept within specified hours of the night, and who also noted the time taken by each patient to get to sleep after the administration of the drug, and any breaks in sleep that occurred. In addition the patients were seen each morning by a doctor who obtained reports from them about the quality of their sleep, and noted any hang-over effects. Several different measurements of the effects of a treatment are desirable if cross-checks are to be made on the reliability of the information. Different measures may reveal different aspects of the effects of the treatments, or side-effects, which may be important in making decisions about the use of the treatments.

Reliability and Validity

Reliability

A measuring instrument, whatever its nature, is said to be reliable if it gives closely similar answers when applied more than once, under similar conditions, to the same person or object whose state is not different on the separate occasions. In the so-called exact sciences, measurements can often be made with great reliability and precision: for instance it was recently shown that the legal British yard differed by about three parts in one million from the legal U.S. yard; even this slight discrepancy had proved to be a nuisance in the interchange of instruments between the two countries and had to be corrected. But in the behavioural sciences, for example in the field of mental testing, and in psychiatric and sociological work in which rating scales, questionnaires and other similar devices are used, the degree of precision possible in the measurements is at a much more molar level. Even the most reliable tests of intelligence so far constructed yield results which are dependable only within limits as much as ten or more points of I.Q. apart. (What is worse, it is hard to see how, in the light of present knowledge, a greater degree of precision can be achieved.) It follows that many of the measuring instruments employed in the behavioural sciences have fairly low reliability. Consequently, it is wise when using such instruments to obtain replicated readings when possible so that information is available about the amount of variability involved. But replication may be difficult. For instance, if a test such as a cognitive test is administered to a subject more than once, with only a short time interval, he may remember the answers to the items or may improve his performance as a result of practice with that particular type of test. The difficulty is in part overcome if a parallel form of the test or inventory is available, though this is seldom the case. However, things are not as hopeless as at first they might appear for there are today satisfactory statistical ways of taking practice effect and trends in repeat measurements into account.

When discussing reliability it is well to be clear about the types of variation which may be affecting a particular measurement process. One type is what is known as *random error*, generally attributed to the numerous small, undefined and uncontrollable factors present when a measurement is made – slight fluctuations in the calibration of an instrument, or slight changes in temperature, humidity, etc., are examples. Similarly, in mental testing random error might be due to lapses of attention, fatigue, interruption, or to the host of other small stimuli by which a human subject is constantly being bombarded. In psychometric work such random disturbing influences are traditionally referred to as 'errors of measurement'. This source of variation is what we have in mind when we talk about reliability, and it must be distinguished from other sources of variation such as variability due to differences between the several subjects in a sample, or differences between the conditions, environmental or imposed, under which the measurements are made.

Published tests for assessing cognitive ability and attainment, and inventories for measuring aspects of personality, etc., invariably have an index of their reliability quoted in the form of a 'reliability coefficient'. Nowadays such coefficients are generally derived by rather elaborate analysis of variance procedures (see Maxwell and Pilliner, 1968). But for tests or inventories consisting of lists of items or questions which are scored dichotomously, that is scored 1 for correct and 0 for incorrect, or 1 for 'agree' and 0 for 'disagree', etc., a well-known and relatively simple method of deriving a reliability coefficient is available.

Suppose that we have a cognitive test made up of $2N$ dichoto-mously scored items; then by taking the odd and the even items separately, the complete test, after it has been administered to a sample of people, can be subdivided into two subtests of N items each, and a score for each person on each subtest can be obtained. Odd and even items are taken separately on the assumption that since they are adjacent in the test they are both likely to have been answered by the testee under con-ditions – environmental and human – which were similar. In other words the two subtests are considered to be parallel forms of one and the same test. The scores for the testees on the two subtests are then correlated (see chapter 7). Let us denote this correlation by $r_{\frac{1}{2}\frac{1}{2}}$, where $\frac{1}{2}$ indicates that the correlation is derived from two subtests each only one half the length of the complete test. The correlation, $r_{\frac{1}{2}\frac{1}{2}}$, is then corrected for length by applying the Spearman–Brown formula (see Lord and Novick, 1968), and an estimate, r_{11}, of the reliability of the full-length test is obtained. The formula is

$$r_{11} = \frac{2r_{\frac{1}{2}\frac{1}{2}}}{1+r_{\frac{1}{2}\frac{1}{2}}}. \qquad 2.3$$

For standardized tests of cognitive ability, such as those con-structed at Moray House or by the National Foundation for Educational Research, the reliabilities are generally as high as 0·95, but to achieve values as high as this the criteria outlined above for item analysis have to be strictly applied.

On the assumption that the means and standard deviations (see chapter 3) of the subtest scores are equal, the reliability coefficient of a test gives an indication of the agreement we might expect to find between subjects' scores on the test as a whole were it possible to administer it to them a second time under similar conditions, and in the absence of practice or other 'carry-over' effects. But the real importance of the reliability coefficient is that it can be used to estimate the margin of error associated with the score obtained by a particular individual on the test. This measure is known as the 'error of measurement' of an obtained score and it is calculated by the formula

Error of measurement $= s\sqrt{(1 - r_{11})}$, **2.4**

where s is an estimate of the standard deviation of the scores on the test in the population of people tested.

Examination of formula **2.4** shows that the nearer r_{11} is to unity, the smaller the error of measurement will be. In other words the reliability of a test must be close to unity if we are to have much confidence in the scores we obtain by administering it. As will be seen in chapter 4, the error of measurement can be employed to set up 'confidence intervals' for an obtained score. Finally it should be mentioned that the reliability coefficient of a test can be increased by increasing the length of the test, and for this reason most standardized tests have as many as 100 items.

Validity

Compared with reliability, the *validity* of a measuring instrument is a much more difficult property to assess. Validity may be defined (somewhat circularly) as the extent to which a measuring instrument measures what it is supposed to measure. In psychological work, where the clear definition of variables is virtually impossible, one has to depend largely on finding an outside criterion against which the measuring instrument can be verified. For instance, if part of the selection process for university students is a battery of standardized intelligence tests, then a possible criterion might be the grades obtained by the students in their degree examinations. Again the validity of a scale for measuring a variable such as 'depression' might be checked by correlating patients' scores on the scale with ratings of depression given to them by experienced consultants. Reliability and validity are not independent concepts, for if a measuring instrument is unreliable this is likely to affect adversely an index of its validity. On the other hand good reliability does not ensure good validity. It is well known that colleagues in an X-ray department may, over a period of time, come to agree very closely with each other in their diagnosis of tuberculosis based on chest X-ray negatives. If the information contained in the negatives were adequate for a full diagnosis then the results might be valid as well as being reliable, but experience has shown that it is not.

Agreement between raters

Sometimes the word 'reliability' is used to indicate 'agreement'. For instance two doctors may interview a patient and each may check a prearranged schedule of symptoms indicating which ones in their opinion are present and which absent. Recently the Maudsley–Bethlem Hospital Item Sheet was filled in, for each patient in a sample of 66, by the registrar in charge of the case and by a senior registrar well acquainted with it. For the symptom 'guilt, self-reproach and unworthiness', the following results were obtained:

		Senior registrar		
		0	*1*	
Registrar	*0*	32	3	35
	1	6	25	31
		38	28	66

where 1 and 0 indicate respectively that the symptom is 'present' or 'absent'. On the basis of the results one might say that this symptom is reasonably 'reliable' since the raters are in agreement for 57 out of the 66 patients, i.e. 86 per cent of the time.

Instead of the percentage agreement it is common practice to give measures of the correlation, and bias if it exists, between the two raters, but these will be discussed later (see chapter 7). Good agreement between the raters does not, of course, imply that the information they give is necessarily valid, but for the example given it does suggest that the raters are interpreting the wording of the item in a similar way and are applying it similarly.

3 Some Simple Descriptive Statistics

Measures of Central Tendency

It has been noted that one of the purposes of statistics is to indicate how results obtained from an experiment or investigation may be described in a concise way. Some common descriptive measures will now be introduced.

Suppose for example that a scale for measuring anxiety or some other such variable has been constructed, say in the manner discussed in chapter 2, and that it is administered to a sample of 20 patients yielding the following 20 scores:

8 6 5 4 5 3 5 9 8 4
6 5 3 2 1 5 4 6 7 7

Now with a very small sample one might report all the scores and leave the reader to assess the results for himself. But this would be unhelpful and it is preferable to try to summarize the data in some way. One useful approach is to count how many scores of each size have been observed (for our example there is one score of size 9, two of size 8, and so on). The results can then be arranged in a *frequency distribution* as follows:

Score (X)	Frequency (f)
9	1
8	2
7	2
6	3
5	5
4	3
3	2
2	1
1	1
	$N = \overline{20}$

If the range of scores is wide it is advisable first to arrange them in *intervals* of a suitable size, such as scores 1 to 4, 5 to 9, etc., and to count how many scores fall into each interval. A partial check on the tabulation is that the total of the column of frequencies should equal the sample size.

If the column of frequencies in our example is examined, it is seen that the score 5 occurs most commonly and that the frequency of other scores, whether above or below 5, tends to occur less often as we move away from 5. In other words the distribution of scores tends to be symmetrical. This can be readily seen if the scores are arranged in a *histogram*, in which the frequency of scores of a given size is represented by the height of a column with the score at the *centre* of its base. For our sample of 20 scores the histogram is given in Figure 1 and the tendency towards symmetry of the distribution is now clear to the eye. For future reference it is important to note that the area enclosed by the histogram represents the sample size.

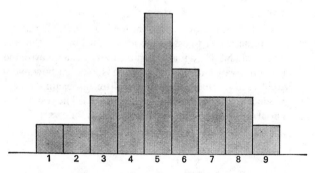

Figure 1 Histogram of 20 scores on an anxiety scale

The most frequently occurring score in a distribution is called the *mode*, and when describing a distribution the mode is often quoted as a *measure of central tendency or location* of the scores as a whole. It is clearly a useful summary statistic when the distribution is reasonably symmetric and has a single peak: the distribution of scores is then said to be *unimodal*.

The mode has the disadvantage that it is generally based on a single score only. In view of this, a more commonly used measure of central tendency is the average or *arithmetic mean* of the scores because it takes them all into account. The sum of the 20 scores given above is 103, so the mean is 103/20 = 5·15. If we use the variable X to indicate the scores, and X_i to indicate the ith score, then a formula for the mean, $\bar{X}$, is

$$\bar{X} = \frac{\sum_{i=1}^{N} X_i}{N}, \cdot \qquad \qquad 3.1$$

in which i runs from 1 to N, or 1 to 20 in our example, and the Greek letter Σ (sigma) indicates 'sum of'.

When a calculating machine is available, the sum of the scores can easily be found by straight addition, otherwise it may be more convenient to find it from the frequency distribution by weighting the scores by their frequency of occurrence. The sum is then given by

$$\text{Sum} = \Sigma f_i X_i,$$

where f_i is the frequency of the ith score. For our example

$$\Sigma f_i X_i = (9 \times 1) + (8 \times 2) + \ldots + (1 \times 1) = 103,$$

which is the total found by straight addition.

As with the mode, the mean of a set of scores is a satisfactory measure of central tendency when the distribution of scores is symmetrical. When it is not, a third measure called the *median* is frequently quoted. It is the score below which half the members of the sample lie, and for our example it is approximately 5. In brief, when a distribution of scores is unimodal and symmetric the mode, mean and median are equal. When a distribution of scores is unsymmetric, it is often possible to reduce the asymmetry by some transformation of the scale of measurement; this is clearly legitimate if the scale itself has been arbitrarily chosen in the first instance. Non-symmetric distributions often occur. A common example is the time taken for a subject to solve a problem such as a test item. If he sees the answer immediately the time to respond is short, but if he has to think about the problem time marches on. Here, for instance, are the times in seconds taken by 13 subjects to answer an item in a test of mental speed:

Subjects

	1	2	3	4	5	6	7	8	9	10	11	12	13	Total
Times	7	5	10	5	2	32	4	1	4	18	8	14	5	115

The median of these scores is roughly 6 seconds while their mean is 8·85 seconds. The latter is unduly influenced by the two relatively extreme scores, 18 and 32, and is biased in their direction.

As an alternative to drawing a histogram, especially when the sample size is small, the distribution of a set of scores can readily be examined by representing them as a series of dots plotted on graph paper. For the 13 scores above, the plot is shown in Figure 2 and the skewness is immediately obvious.

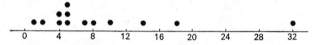

Figure 2 Distribution of 13 time scores in seconds

If the logarithms (to any base) of these scores are now obtained and plotted, the effect of the positive skewness is in large measure eliminated. The transformed scores, using logarithms to the base 10, are

0·845, 0·699, 1·000, 0·699, 0·301, 1·505, 0·602
0·000, 0·602, 1·255, 0·903, 1·146, 0·699,

and their distribution is given in Figure 3.

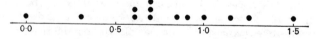

Figure 3 Distribution of the logarithms of the 13 time scores

The distribution is now much less skewed. Moreover, the mean of the logarithms is 0·789, which, when converted back to raw scores, is 6·15 seconds – a value which agrees well with the median and is more representative of the observed scores than the mean value 8·85 obtained before the transformation.

Measures of Dispersion

It has now been shown that useful summary statistics for describing a set of data are the mean, median and mode. But on their own these measures are not sufficient, for they are concerned only with 'location' and provide no information about the spread or variability of the data. For instance, if we examine the following two samples, each containing 4 scores,

Sample	Scores	Mean
I	6, 4, 7, 5	5·5
II	7, 10, 1, 4	5·5

it is seen that they each have a mean of 5·5, but the samples are still very different for in the first the scores have little variability whereas in the second they vary considerably. A commonly used measure of variability in a sample of scores, or other measures, is their *range*. It is the difference between the largest and smallest scores in a sample. For the data above the ranges are

Sample I	$7-4 = 3$
Sample II	$10-1 = 9$

and these measures indicate the difference in variability of the scores in the two samples.

The range is a useful measure of variability, especially when we have a lot of relatively small samples of equal size; but it has the limitation that it is based on just two scores and so may give a very biased impression of variability if either the smallest or largest score in the sample happens to be an outlier. Partly for this reason a more commonly used measure of variability of a sample of scores is their *standard deviation*; in common with the mean, it takes all the scores in the sample into account.

The calculation of the standard deviation is a bit cumbersome but this measure, and its square which is known as the *variance*, have several attractive mathematical and sampling properties which account for their favour amongst statisticians.

To find the variance of a set of scores we first subtract the mean from each. The resulting scores, or deviations from the mean, will then be roughly half positive and half negative and they add to zero. The deviations are then squared (which eliminates the negative signs), added and divided by $N-1$, where N is the sample size. This gives an estimate of the variance of the scores in the population from which the sample is drawn, and its square root is their standard deviation. If we denote the raw scores by X_i and their deviations from their mean by x_i, the calculation can be written symbolically as follows

$$\text{Sum of squares of deviations} = \sum_{i=1}^{N} x_i^2 = \sum_{i=1}^{N} (X_i - \overline{X})^2. \qquad 3.3$$

This calculation can be performed more easily if we note that algebraically

$$\sum (X_i - \overline{X})^2 = \sum X_i^2 - \frac{(\sum X_i)^2}{N}. \qquad 3.4$$

Let us denote the variance of the scores by s^2, then the formula required is

$$s^2 = \frac{\sum x_i^2}{N-1} \qquad 3.5$$

and the standard deviation s is obtained by taking the square root, so that

$$s = \sqrt{\frac{\sum x_i^2}{N-1}}. \qquad 3.6$$

To illustrate the calculations we may take the sample of 20 anxiety scores discussed earlier; they are

8	6	5	4	5	3	5	9	8	4
6	5	3	2	1	5	4	6	7	7.

The quantities required are
(i) the sum of the scores

$$\Sigma X = 103,$$

(ii) the sum of the squares of the scores

$$\Sigma X^2 = 8^2 + 6^2 + \ldots + 7^2 = 611,$$

(iii) the sum of squares of the deviations of the scores from the mean, given by

$$\Sigma x^2 = \Sigma X^2 - \frac{(\Sigma X)^2}{N}$$

$$= 611 - \frac{103^2}{20}$$

$$= 80 \cdot 55.$$

The estimate of the variance of the scores is then

$$s^2 = \frac{\Sigma x^2}{N-1} = \frac{80 \cdot 55}{19} = 4 \cdot 24,$$

and the standard deviation is the square root of this, namely,

$$s = \sqrt{4 \cdot 24} = 2 \cdot 06.$$

It is important to note that the standard deviation is in the same units as the original scores.

The scores for the 20 patients on the anxiety scale might now be described by the following summary statistics:

Sample size $N = 20$
Mean $\overline{X} = 5 \cdot 15$
Standard deviation $s = 2 \cdot 06.$

But the question immediately arises as to how adequate a description of the data these measures provide. To answer this question it will be necessary to describe a distribution very widely used in statistical work, namely the *normal distribution*. But before doing so a few technical terms are needed.

Some Technical Terms

The word *population* is used in statistics to indicate any well-defined class of people, animals, objects, etc. Sometimes the class is finite and numerable, such as the number of males on any given week receiving old-age pensions in the Isle of Man; but more often it is hypothetical. For instance, when we speak of the class of patients diagnosed as 'catatonic schizophrenics', we generally have in mind patients past, present and future suffering from this illness. Now when we come to measure people belonging to some population on a given variable, it is usually impossible to measure all of them; we have to be content with a sample. It follows that the results we obtain will reflect the magnitude and variability of the variable in the population only to the extent that the sample is a truly representative cross-section of the population.

A great deal of the mathematical theory of statistics assumes the existence of populations and further assumes that for any given variable 'true' values of measures such as its mean, or variance, exist. These 'true' values are called *parameters*, but they are seldom exactly known. To distinguish them from estimates of them, obtained from a sample, it is customary to refer to them by Greek letters. Hence the mean of a variable in the *population* is typically referred to by the letter μ (mu) and the standard deviation by σ (sigma), the corresponding sample values being denoted by Roman letters such as $\overline{X}$ and s respectively. $\overline{X}$ is then said to be an estimate of μ and s to be an estimate of σ. When samples are fairly large and are truly representative of the population from which they are drawn then it is to be expected that $\overline{X}$ and s will have values closely approximating their population values. With the definitions of μ and σ in mind, we can now describe the normal distribution.

The Normal Distribution

The normal distribution is shown in Figure 4. The base line in the figure represents the scale, or variable, in question, while the height of the curve above any point on the base (that is above any given score) gives the relative density of scores of that magnitude. The curve is symmetrical and unimodal, with its highest point at the mean. The algebraic equation of the curve, which gives the height Y, for any given value of the variable X, is

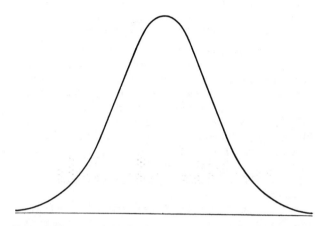

Figure 4 The normal distribution

$$Y = \frac{1}{\sigma\sqrt{(2\pi)}}e^{-(X-\mu)^2/2\sigma^2}.$$ **3.7**

A brief look at this equation is informative, for it throws light on the question posed earlier regarding the number of summary statistics necessary for an adequate description of a sample of data. In the equation the symbols π (pi) and e need not detain us for they are well-known mathematical constants with approximate values 3·142 and 2·718 respectively. Having disposed of them we see that if, for some variable X, μ and σ are known, then the value of Y for any given value of X can immediately be calculated. In other words, the only constants, apart from π and e, in the equation are μ and σ, and if, for a given variable X, μ and σ are known (or, what in practice amounts to the same thing, if good estimates $\overline{X}$ and s of μ and σ are known), then the normal curve is completely determined. This means that if a variable X is normally, or near normally, distributed in some population, an adequate description of a sample of data drawn from that population is provided if we state the mean and the standard deviation. These two measures are said to be *sufficient* statistics for the data. The size of the sample too should always be given as it is required when setting up confidence limits for the mean (see chapter 4).

Tables for the normal distribution

Many variables commonly employed in experimental work are found to be approximately normally distributed, or can be rendered so by some fairly simple transformation. Indeed in many psychological investigations the scale on which a variable is to be measured is often arbitrary and so can frequently be chosen in such a way that a normal distribution of scores is obtained. Possible skewness in a distribution of scores on a cognitive test, too, can often be foreseen and prevented by the inclusion of further items of greater or less difficulty as the situation may demand, and so on.

But each variable employed in an investigation will have its own individual values of $\bar{X}$ and s, probably all different and expressed in terms of the particular units of measurement peculiar to each. However, all can be put on a comparable scale if we replace the observed scores on each variable by their standardized equivalents. The transformation required is

$$z_i = \frac{X_i - \mu}{\sigma}, \qquad\qquad 3.8$$

where X_i is an observed score for a normally distributed variable with mean μ and standard deviation σ. It can be shown that these z-scores have a mean of *zero* and a standard deviation of *unity*, and this will be so whatever the units (inches, grammes, etc.) used when measuring the variable in question. The equation of the normal curve, using z rather than X as the observed variable, now takes the simpler form

$$y = \frac{1}{\sqrt{(2\pi)}} e^{-\frac{1}{2}z^2}. \qquad\qquad 3.9$$

When this expression is used the area (Figure 4) between the curve and the base line is unity and by analogy with a histogram, this area now corresponds to the size of the population. Moreover, tables have been prepared (Appendix 1) from which we can read off, for any given value of z, the proportions into which the total area bounded by the curve is divided by a vertical line drawn at that value of z. This means that we can read off the proportion of people in our population who may be expected to have scores above or below a given value.

Let us see, by means of an example, some of the ways in which these tables can be used. Suppose we take a test, or other measuring device, on which scores for a given population are normally distributed, and for which μ and σ, or good estimates of them, are known. The Wechsler Adult Intelligence Scale is an example and it is reasonable to assume that it has $\mu = 100$ and $\sigma = 15$. Now suppose we wish to know what proportion of the population we would expect to have I.Q.s, as provided by this test, equal to or less than the value 120. We first express $X = 120$ in z-form using equation **3.8** and find

$$z = \frac{120 - 100}{15} = 1\cdot33.$$

We now refer this z-value to the tables (Appendix 1) and find, corresponding to it, the proportion 0·9082. This is the proportion of the area of the normal curve below a z-value of 1·33, or equivalently below an X-value of 120. We can immediately say that for this test we would expect 90·82 per cent of the population to have I.Q.s less than or equal to 120.

Now suppose we wish to know what percentage of the population we would expect to have I.Q.s lying between 85 and 120. The z-value for 85 is

$$z = \frac{85 - 100}{15} = -1\cdot00.$$

The tables do not give proportions for negative values, but since the normal curve is symmetrical about its mean we can look up $z = +1\cdot00$ instead. For $z = 1\cdot00$ the tables give the proportion 0·8413, so that $z = -1\cdot0$ cuts off a tail of the curve on the left hand side of area: $1 - 0\cdot8413 = 0\cdot1587$. It follows that 15·87 per cent of the population have I.Q.s less than or equal to 85, hence the percentage with I.Q.s lying between 120 and 85 is

$$90 \cdot 82\% - 15 \cdot 87\% = 74 \cdot 95\%.$$

The normal distribution has many uses in statistical theory other than those just mentioned. One of them is concerned with the accuracy of an estimate of a population mean and is discussed in the next chapter.

4 Elementary Sampling Theory

The Accuracy of an Estimate of a Population Mean

We have seen that many of the populations with which research workers are concerned are either hypothetical or are so large that an investigation has to be carried out on a sample only. From the sample, estimates of population parameters, such as μ and σ, for each of the several variables being measured are derived. Clearly, the amount of credence that can be placed in the estimates will depend on factors such as the degree to which the sample is representative of the population, the extent to which assumptions, such as the assumption of normality, are met, and of course on the size of the sample used. We shall now consider the latter point and see how the accuracy of the estimate of a mean depends on the size of the sample.

When an estimate of the magnitude of some quantity is made, it is good statistical practice to accompany it by an estimate of the amount of variation to expect should further determinations of that magnitude, under similar conditions, be carried out. In the case of a mean this estimate is known as the standard error of the mean and it is derived by considering the *sampling distribution* of the mean. Let us refer again to the investigation of London school children aged eleven years. There it is stated that the mean weight for a sample of 336 boys from one-child families is $37 \cdot 01 \pm 0 \cdot 36$ kg. In this statement the quantity $0 \cdot 36$ is the standard error (standard deviation of the sampling distribution) of the mean. The problem is to see how it is derived and interpreted.

The theory on which the estimate of the standard error of a mean is based is as follows. The size of the sample used in the determination of the children's weights was 336 and the mean obtained was 37·01. Now let us assume that many more random samples of size 336 are drawn from the same population of boys and the mean weight for each sample ascertained. Practical experience shows that the means of these additional samples would not all be exactly 37·01. Some might be larger and some smaller. If we had the means of many samples each of 336 cases, we could plot these sample means in the form of a histogram. Whenever this has been done, it is found that the histogram tends to be symmetric about the mean of the sample means and to approximate the normal distribution. Certain theoretical considerations lead one to expect this tendency; the mathematical theorem concerned is known as the *central limit theorem*. This theorem applies strictly only where the distribution of the variable in the population being sampled is normal. However, the tendency for the distributions of sample means to be normal also exists, with a few exceptions, where the population distribution of the variable is not normal. This remarkable fact is the principal reason for the leading role which the normal distribution plays in statistical theory. The reader can easily check this tendency towards normality for himself by throwing dice. If a single unbiased die is thrown a large number of times we would expect the faces 1, 2, . . ., 6 to occur about equally frequently and a histogram of the results would tend to be rectangular in shape. But if several unbiased dice are thrown simultaneously and the mean or average of the sum of the faces that occurs on each throw is found, the histogram of these averages will tend strongly to normality. For instance the writer threw 4 dice 342 times and the distribution for the averages of the results of the throws is shown in Figure 5.

The Standard Error of a Mean

The standard error of a mean is defined as the standard deviation of a distribution of means for an infinite set of samples of the same size drawn randomly from the same population. Luckily the experiment does not have to be performed to get an estimate of the standard error, for it can be shown that for a

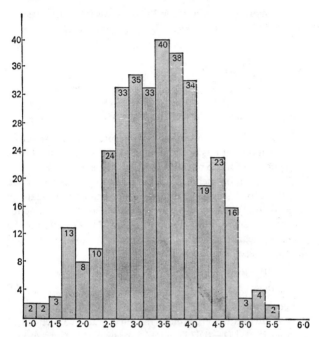

Figure 5 Histogram for the averages of 4 dice thrown
342 times

variable with known standard deviation, σ, the standard error
of the mean (σ_{mean}) for samples of size N is given by

$$\sigma_{\text{mean}} = \frac{\sigma}{\sqrt{N}}. \qquad \qquad 4.1$$

If only an estimate s of σ is known then the formlua for estimating the standard error of the mean is

$$s_{\text{mean}} = \frac{s}{\sqrt{N}}. \qquad \qquad 4.2$$

We can now see how the value 0·36 in the expression for the
boys' weights, namely $37\cdot01 \pm 0\cdot36$, was obtained. The standard

deviation of the weights of the 336 boys was found using equation **3.6** to be $(s =) 6.60$ kg so that, by equation **4.2**,

$$s_{mean} = \frac{6.60}{\sqrt{336}} = 0.36.$$

Interpreting the Standard Error of the Mean

The next problem is how to use and interpret the standard error of a mean once it has been found. For this purpose the tables (Appendix 1) for the normal distribution are required.

The population mean, μ, of the boys' weights is unknown, but from our sample we have an estimate of it, namely $\bar{X} = 37.01$. We have also an estimate, 0.36, of the standard error of the distribution of sample means. The deviation of the observed mean from the population mean can now be expressed in standardized form (equation **3.8**), as

$$z = \frac{37.01 - \mu}{0.36}. \qquad \qquad 4.3$$

Let us now turn to the tables. There we find that a z-value of 1.96 divides the area under the curve into two sections of area 0.975 and $(1 - 0.975 =) 0.025$, respectively. Correspondingly, a z-value of -1.96 divides the area into sections of size 0.025 and 0.975 respectively. In other words a proportion $(1 - 2 \times 0.025 =) 0.950$, or 95 per cent, of the curve lies between z-values of -1.96 and $+1.96$. This is shown in Figure 6. In other words, the value of z lies between -1.96 and $+1.96$ for 95 per cent of the time. Using expression **4.3** we may thus write

$$1.96 \geqslant \frac{37.01 - \mu}{0.36} > -1.96.$$

This can be written more simply as

$37.01 + 1.96 \times 0.36 \geqslant \mu > 37.01 - 1.96 \times 0.36,$

or $\qquad 37.01 + 0.71 \geqslant \mu > 37.01 - 0.71,$

or $\qquad \qquad 37.72 \geqslant \mu > 36.30.$

But it is unnecessary to go through this elaborate calculation on

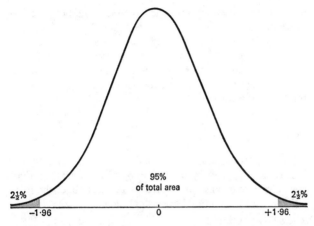

Figure 6 The normal distribution

each occasion, for the 95 per cent limits are given by the expression

$$\overline{X} \pm 1 \cdot 96 \, s_{mean} \qquad \text{4.4}$$

for relatively large values of N.

Hence we can say, with a 95 per cent chance of being correct, that the true mean of boys' weights lies in the interval 37·72 kg to 36·30 kg. Had we wished to make a statement with confidence greater than 95 per cent, say 99 per cent, then we would refer to the tables and find the z-value which cuts off tails of area 0·005 each. It is $z = 2 \cdot 58$ and in our calculations we would use this value in place of $z = 1 \cdot 96$; the limits would now be slightly further apart.

The limits or bounds for the true mean given above are known as *fiducial limits* and the methods by which they are derived was first given by R. A. Fisher. Limits of equal size can also be derived by an argument based on the idea of repeated sampling. They are called *confidence limits* and the statement then made is that in repeated sampling, with $N = 336$, we would expect the sample means to lie between 37·72 kg and 36·30 kg 95 per cent of the time in the long run. Fortunately, for elementary work it is immaterial which approach is used since both give the same answer.

The width of the confidence limits indicates the accuracy of the estimate of the mean derived from the sample. The closer the limits the more accurate the estimate is. One way of reducing the width is to reduce the size of the standard error of the mean, and since the formula is

$$s_{mean} = \frac{s}{\sqrt{N}}$$

this can be achieved by increasing the sample size. Indeed, as N is increased, $s_{mean} \rightarrow 0$, so that the confidence limits eventually coincide. This makes sense, for the true mean, μ, of the population must by definition have a single definite value.

The t-Distribution

Before leaving our discussion of confidence limits, one further point of detail must be considered. In many experiments, and perhaps especially in medical experiments, the number of patients involved is often rather small – usually considerably below 60. Under these conditions use of the normal distribution can be misleading in cases where σ is unknown. In short whereas the expression

$$z = \frac{\overline{X} - \mu}{\sigma/\sqrt{N}} \qquad \textbf{4.5}$$

is normally distributed, the expression

$$t = \frac{\overline{X} - \mu}{s/\sqrt{N}} \qquad \textbf{4.6}$$

for small N is not. It has a different distribution for each different value of N, or, more precisely, for different *degrees of freedom* as they are called, the latter being given by $N-1$.

A table of the t-distribution for different degrees of freedom is given in Appendix 2. To show how the table is used, let us set up 95 per cent confidence limits for the mean score obtained with a sample of 20 patients on the anxiety scale discussed in chapters 2 and 3.

The data are

$$N = 20; \qquad \bar{X} = 5 \cdot 15; \qquad s = 2 \cdot 06.$$

An estimate of the standard error of the mean can be found using equation 4.2. It is

$$s_{\text{mean}} = \frac{2 \cdot 06}{\sqrt{20}} = 0 \cdot 46.$$

In the case of the normal distribution, 95 per cent of the area under the curve was seen to be included between the values $z = \pm 1 \cdot 96$. But since our sample size is small (only 20) we must now refer to the *t*-distribution with $N - 1$ or 19 degrees of freedom (d.f.). First we locate the row for 19 d.f. (or one close to it) and read the entry for the column headed 0·05 (i.e. 5 per cent); it is approximately 2·09. The *z*-values we require are then $\pm 2 \cdot 09$, rather than $\pm 1 \cdot 96$, and the 95 per cent confidence limits are

$$(5 \cdot 15 + 2 \cdot 09 \times 0 \cdot 46) \quad \text{and} \quad (5 \cdot 15 - 2 \cdot 09 \times 0 \cdot 46),$$
namely   6·11   and   4·19.

These are very far apart and indicate that in repeated testing with random samples of size only 20, the mean score on the scale would be likely to vary considerably. To improve the situation a sample of larger size would be required.

5 Elementary Concepts of Probability

Introduction

Statistical theory borrows heavily from the theory of mathematical probability and in this chapter some elementary concepts from the latter will be introduced.

Questions of probability were first studied seriously by mathematicians in the seventeenth and eighteenth centuries and were initially concerned with problems which arose in games of chance. But interest in the subject was aroused again in this century as the science of statistics developed and statistical inference assumed new importance.

Questions of probability arise in situations in which there is uncertainty. We are all aware of them in everyday life. For instance when a baby is about to be born we speculate about the possibility of its being a boy or a girl, and know from experience that the chances are about even. However, if we wanted to be more precise we might look up some records. For example, of the 785 005 babies born in 1960 in Great Britain, 404 150 were boys. This gives the proportion of boys and girls to be 0·515 and 0·485 respectively so that, other things being equal, the baby is slightly more likely to be a boy than a girl.

It is interesting to consider the types of evidence on which statements of probability are based. They may be based on general experience, as when we say that the chances of a baby being a boy or girl are about even. But they may also be based on census or other published data, as was the case when we looked up records of the actual number of boys and girls born in a specific period. Again, they may result from a deliberate investigation. For instance, on the basis of several prospective studies, it is now known that the probabilities of a baby having congenital cataract if the mother contracts rubella during the first or second four weeks of pregnancy are about 0·5 and 0·25 respectively.

But in many situations, for instance those concerned with coin-tossing or throwing dice, probability statements are often based on the concept of symmetry or of equal likelihood. Few of us have ever owned an octahedron, but if given a regular octahedron we would be prepared to guess that, if thrown, each of its eight faces would be equally likely to appear uppermost. To demonstrate the fact we would of course have to throw the octahedron a large number of times and record the results. Even if we did we could never be sure about the true probabilities of the different faces, but if their relative frequencies approached equality, before the octahedron itself became too worn, we would conclude that the octahedron was unbiased.

Much of the elementary theory of probability can be illustrated by throwing coins or dice, but mention must first be made of two elementary laws of probability.

The Addition and Multiplication Laws of Probability

The *addition law* of probability states that if A and B are mutually exclusive events, that is events both of which cannot occur simultaneously, then the probability that either A *or* B will occur is equal to the sum of their separate probabilities.

To illustrate the point, suppose that we are given a fair die. Then we would expect each face to occur one sixth of the time in the long run if the die were thrown; in other words we could say that the probability of each face occuring is $\frac{1}{6}$. Now when a die is thrown on a flat surface and comes to rest only one face can be uppermost, so that the possibility of any one face occurring on a single trial excludes the possibility of any other face occurring on that trial, the events throwing a 1, throwing a 2, etc., are mutually exclusive. It is clear then that the probability of getting a 1 (event A, say) or a 2 (event B) is the sum of the probability of each, namely

$$\frac{1}{6} + \frac{1}{6} = \frac{1}{3},$$

that is   Prob(A *or* B) = Prob(A) + Prob(B).

The rule can be extended to more than two events: for example, for three mutually exclusive events A, B and C

Prob(A *or* B *or* C) = Prob(A)+Prob(B)+Prob(C).

The *multiplication law* of probability states that if two events are independent (the occurrence of one in no way affects the occurrence of the other) then the probability of both occurring is the product of the probability of each. Written symbolically we have

Prob(A *and* B) = Prob(A)×Prob(B).

For example, if two unbiased coins are tossed, then the probability of getting two heads is

$\frac{1}{2} \times \frac{1}{2} = \frac{1}{4}$,

since the probability of a head for each is $\frac{1}{2}$. On the other hand the probability of getting a head and a tail is $\frac{1}{2}$. This is so because we can get a head with the first coin and a tail with the second with probability

$\frac{1}{2} \times \frac{1}{2} = \frac{1}{4}$,

but equally we can get a tail with the first coin and a head with the second, again with probability

$\frac{1}{2} \times \frac{1}{2} = \frac{1}{4}$.

And since either of these two mutually exclusive events provides the outcome required, the results can be added to give the probability of a head and a tail when two coins are tossed, namely

$\frac{1}{4} + \frac{1}{4} = \frac{1}{2}$.

The Binomial Distribution

Knowledge of the addition and multiplication laws of probability enables us immediately to discuss a distribution much used in statistical work, namely the *binomial distribution*.

Suppose a jar contains N balls of which a proportion p is black and a proportion q is white, where $p+q = 1$. We shake the jar, draw a ball from it, note its colour and replace it. We then repeat the procedure a second time. The result of these two trials (which we will call the event) has four possible outcomes. These are shown in the first column of Table 1 (where W indicates a white, and B a black ball).

Table 1
Probability of Events Involving Two Balls

Balls	Event	Probability	Combining similar events
Both black	B B	p^2	p^2
Black and white	B W	pq	$\left.\right\}\ 2pq$
White and black	W B	qp	
Both white	W W	q^2	q^2

Since the probability of drawing a black ball is p, the probability of drawing two black balls on one trial is $p \times p = p^2$. Again the probability of drawing a white ball is q, hence the probability of the event BW is pq and of the event WB is qp. Finally, the probability of the event WW is q^2. The total probability of the four events is

$$p^2 + 2pq + q^2 = (p+q)^2 = 1, \quad \text{since } (p+q) = 1.$$

If each event consists of the drawing of three balls then the possible outcomes are greater, for with BB we can have a B or a W, giving BBB or BBW. Again with BW we can have a B or W giving BWB or BWW, etc. The possible outcomes with their associated probabilities are given in Table 2.

Table 2
Probabilities of Events Involving Three Balls

Event	Probabilities	Combining similar events
BBB	p^3	p^3
BBW	p^2q*	
BWB	p^2q*	$3p^2q*$
BWW	pq^2**	
WBB	p^2q*	
WBW	pq^2**	$3pq^2**$
WWB	pq^2**	
WWW	q^3	q^3

Again we can show that the sum of the probabilities of the eight (2^3) possible outcomes or events is unity, for

$$p^3 + 3p^2q + 3pq^2 + q^3 = (p+q)^3 = 1, \quad \text{since } (p+q) = 1.$$

A general rule can now be written down for the probabilities of the possible outcomes when the events consist of the drawing with replacement of 4, 5 or more balls on each occasion. For example, if the event consists of the drawing of 4 balls with replacement on each trial, the binomial distribution required is

$$(p+q)^4 = p^4 + 4p^3q + 6p^2q^2 + 4pq^3 + q^4 = 1.$$

In this distribution p^4 gives the probability of drawing 4 black balls, that is of the event BBBB. The quantity $4p^3q$ is the probability of drawing 3 black balls and 1 white in any order, say BBBW or BWBB, etc. Similarly, the probability of drawing two black and two white balls is the term $6p^2q^2$, and so on. Note that the index of p tells us the number of black balls and the index of q the number of white balls in the event, so that the probability $4pq^3$ refers to situations in which we have one black ball and three white balls.

The coefficients in the expansion of $(p+q)^n$, where the event consists of n balls, can be written in terms of combinations as follows

$$(p+q)^n = p^n + {}_nC_1\,p^{n-1}q + {}_nC_2\,p^{n-2}q^2 + \ldots,$$

where ${}_nC_1 = n$,

$${}_nC_2 = \frac{n(n-1)}{1 \times 2},$$

$${}_nC_3 = \frac{n(n-1)(n-2)}{1 \times 2 \times 3},$$

etc.

They can also be got using Pascal's triangle as shown below:

```
      1   1                    (p+q)¹
    1   2   1                  (p+q)²
  1   3   3   1                (p+q)³
1   4   6   4   1              (p+q)⁴
      etc.
```

in which each row of the triangle begins (and ends) with 1 and is followed (or preceded) by a term which is the sum of the two terms either side of it in the row above.

Uses of the Binomial Distribution

The binomial distribution can often be employed to assess results obtained in an experiment. Suppose that there is a standard treatment A for a given disease, but it is thought that a new treatment B would be more effective. An experiment to test this claim could be designed as follows. Patients for inclusion in it are matched in pairs and one of each pair is randomly assigned to have treatment A while the other has B. Let us suppose that for a sample of 12 pairs of patients treatment B is found to be preferable to A in 10 cases. The binomial expression in which we would now be interested is

$$(p+q)^{12}$$

and we would want to know the probability of getting 10 (or more) B's in the expansion of this expression. The first four terms of the expansion are

$$p^{12} + 12p^{11}q + 66p^{10}q^2 + 220p^9q^3 \ldots .$$

The first task is to decide what values to ascribe to p and q, where p is taken to be the probability that a patient will do better on B than on A and q is the complementary probability. In the light of having no real factual evidence about B it would appear reasonable in the first instance to take $p = q = \frac{1}{2}$. Here the hypothesis to be tested is that the two treatments are equally effective (the null hypothesis). On this hypothesis we must now calculate the probability of obtaining 10 B's and 2 A's.

The first term, p^{12}, in the expansion refers to the event in which, for all 12 pairs of patients, treatment B is preferred. The second term, $12p^{11}q$ refers to the event in which treatment B is preferred to A for 11 pairs of patients but A is preferred to B for the remaining pair. The third term in the expansion refers to the event in which B is preferred for 10 pairs and A for the remaining two, etc. With $p = q = \frac{1}{2}$ the values of the first four probabilities in the expansion are

$$
\begin{aligned}
p^{12} &= & (\tfrac{1}{2})^{12} &= 0\cdot000244, \\
12p^{11}q &= & 12(\tfrac{1}{2})^{12} &= 0\cdot002928, \\
66p^{10}q^2 &= & 66(\tfrac{1}{2})^{12} &= 0\cdot016104, \\
220p^9q^3 &= & 220(\tfrac{1}{2})^{12} &= 0\cdot053680.
\end{aligned}
$$

The probability $0\cdot016104$ refers to the observed outcome of 10 B's and 2 A's. We can now use these results to introduce the idea of *tests of significance*. The null hypothesis under consideration in our hypothetical experiment is that the two treatments, A and B, are equally effective, that is that $p = q = \frac{1}{2}$. To carry out a test of significance we first decide on an arbitrary value of the probability of the possible outcomes and say that if the observed result is equal to or less than this arbitrary value we will reject the null hypothesis in favour of some other hypothesis, for instance that $p > q$. An arbitrary value frequently used is a probability of $0\cdot05$, known as the 5 per cent level of significance. This value divides the total (unity) of the probabilities of all possible outcomes into two regions, a rejection region of size $0\cdot05$ and an acceptance region of size $0\cdot95$. Now the probabilities given by the expansion of

$$(p+q)^n$$

with $n = 12$ and $p = q = \frac{1}{2}$ have been found to be

$$0\cdot000244 + 0\cdot002928 + 0\cdot016104 + 0\cdot053680 + \ldots.$$

On examining this series we see that the division between the rejection and the acceptance areas lies between the third and fourth terms, for while

$$0\cdot000244 + 0\cdot002928 + 0\cdot016104 < 0\cdot05$$

and so lies in the rejection area, the sum of the first four terms is $0\cdot072956$, which is greater than $0\cdot05$ and so lies in the acceptance area. Consequently, since the first three terms, which include the probability of the observed result of 10 B's and 2 A's, lies in the rejection area we reject the null hypothesis and decide that B is better than A at the 5 per cent level of significance.

One-Tail and Two-Tail Tests

The above test is known as a one-tail test of significance as it was aimed at answering the question, 'Is B more effective than the standard treatment A?' Frequently, however, we may wish to compare two treatments and to decide simply whether either is preferable to the other. In such cases we would be concerned with both tails in the expansion of $(p+q)^n$. Suppose then that in the last experiment we wish to test whether treatments A and B are equally effective. Our rejection area would now involve both tails of the distribution. For $p = q$ the distribution is symmetric and if we wish to make the test at the 5 per cent level of significance the rejection area must include areas of 0·025 in size at each tail of the distribution. The dividing point for our example will again lie between the probabilities 0·016104 and 0·053680 at either end of the distribution since

$$2(0·000244 + 0·002928 + 0·016104) = 0·036552$$

is less than 0·05. Since the probability 0·016104 is the probability that of the 12 possible outcomes 10 are of one kind and 2 of the other, namely the terms $66p^{10}q^2$ or $66p^2q^{10}$ in the expansion of $(p+q)^{12}$, while the other terms included in the rejection area represent more extreme distinctions between the two treatments, we can reject the null hypothesis that the treatments are equally effective.

The Binomial Distribution with Relatively Large *n*

When the sample size *n* in an experiment is large, the determination of the probabilities of the different terms in the expansion of $(p+q)^n$ becomes laborious. This difficulty can be obviated by employing an approximate test. As *n* becomes large, the binomial distribution approximates closely to the normal distribution, even in cases where *p* is not equal to *q*. To use the approximate test we calculate the standardized deviate (*z*) by the formula

$$z = \frac{k - \frac{1}{2}n}{\frac{1}{2}\sqrt{n}} \qquad \textbf{5.1}$$

or more accurately, for relatively small n, by

$$z = \frac{k - \frac{1}{2}n - \frac{1}{2}}{\frac{1}{2}\sqrt{n}}. \qquad 5.2$$

In these expressions n is the number of comparisons made between two treatments, P and S say; $\frac{1}{2}n$ is the expected number of preferences for P or S, on the null hypothesis that they are both equally effective; while k is the number of observed preferences for P or S, whichever is the greater. The value of z is then referred to the normal distribution.

To illustrate the test we will use some results from an experiment in which the relative effectiveness as tranquillizers of sodium amytal (S) and perphenazine (P) were compared. Thirty patients were available for the experiment and they were divided randomly into two groups of 15 patients each. The patients in one group, chosen randomly, were administered drug S for a period of two days and then drug P for a period of two days. There was a two-day interval between the administration of S and P on which drugs were not administered, to guard against carry-over effects. The other group of patients received the drugs in the reverse order. The experiment was conducted as a double-blind trial, neither the patients nor the doctor, who was to assess the relative effects of the drugs, being told which drug was being administered to which group first, though both the patients and the doctor knew that the drugs were different in the two testing sessions. For 3 of the 30 patients no distinction could be made between the relative *merits* of S and P, but for the remaining 27 patients 16 were rated as having fared better on P. The question was to calculate the probability of getting 16 or more preferences out of 27 for either treatment. To do this, using the binomial distribution, would involve quite onerous calculations, but we can instead use expression **5.2**. We have $\frac{1}{2}n = 27/2 = 13\cdot5$; $k = 16$; and $0\cdot5\sqrt{27} = 2\cdot598$,

hence $$z = \frac{16 - 13\cdot5 - 0\cdot5}{2\cdot598} = 0\cdot77. \qquad 5.3$$

If we decide to carry out our test of significance at the 5 per cent level (two-tail) we refer to the table of the normal curve

(Appendix 1) and find the z-values which cut off a proportion 0·025 of the area of the curve in each tail: they are $+1·96$ and $-1·96$. The tail areas now constitute the rejection area for testing the null hypothesis that the two treatments are equivalent (see Figure 6, chapter 4).

Returning to equation **5.3** we have a z-value of 0·77 for the experimental results, and since this is less than 1·96 it lies in the acceptance area, hence we have insufficient evidence to reject the null hypothesis or to claim that S is more effective than P. Here it is advisable to note that the result of the experiment does not allow us to claim that the two treatments are equally effective.

Had we been testing the hypothesis (one-tail) that S is more effective than P, then the critical value of z would have been 1·64 rather than 1·96, for the value of 1·64 cuts off a tail at one end of the distribution with an area of 0·05, corresponding to the 5 per cent level of significance.

Joint and Conditional Probabilities

The addition law of probability, given earlier, which states that the Prob(A *or* B) = Prob(A) + Prob(B) refers to the situation in which A and B are mutually exclusive events. If the events are not mutually exclusive a more elaborate expression is required, namely,

$$\text{Prob(A } or \text{ B)} = \text{Prob(A)} + \text{Prob(B)} - \text{Prob(A } and \text{ B)}. \qquad \textbf{5.4}$$

For example, in throwing a die we might want to know the probability of throwing a number divisible by *either* 2 or 3. In this simple case we know the answer is $\frac{2}{3}$ since any of the four faces 2, 3, 4, 6 meet our requirements and the probability of any one of the four is $\frac{4}{6} = \frac{2}{3}$. However, we can also arrive at this answer by means of equation **5.4**. Let Prob(A) be the probability of throwing a number divisible by 2. This is $\frac{1}{2}$ since any of the three faces 2, 4, 6 fulfils the requirements. Let Prob(B) be the probability of throwing a number divisible by 3. This is $\frac{1}{3}$ since the two faces 3 and 6 fulfil the requirements. However since 6 appears in both Prob(A) and Prob(B), the two events A and B are not mutually exclusive. But we know from the multiplication law that the joint probability of A and B, i.e. Prob(A *and* B), is equal to Prob(A) × Prob(B), which is $\frac{1}{2} \times \frac{1}{3} = \frac{1}{6}$. Substituting these values in equation **5.4** we get

$$\frac{1}{2} + \frac{1}{3} - \frac{1}{6} = \frac{2}{3},$$

which is known to be correct.

The *multiplication law* in its turn needs adjustment if the events A and B are not independent. The formula

$$\text{Prob(A } and \text{ B)} = \text{Prob(A)} \times \text{Prob(B)}$$

becomes $\text{Prob(A } and \text{ B)} = \text{Prob(A)} \times \text{Prob(B|A)},$ **5.5**

where Prob(B|A) stands for the probability of event B given that A has already happened, what is called the *conditional probability* of B given A. For example, what is the probability of obtaining a number divisible by 2 and 3 when throwing a die? We know the answer to be $\frac{1}{6}$ since only one face of the die, namely 6, meets the requirements. To apply formula **5.5** let Prob(A) denote the probability of throwing a number divisible by 2. Three faces of the die, namely, 2, 4 and 6, meet this requirement, hence

$$\text{Prob(A)} = \frac{1}{6} + \frac{1}{6} + \frac{1}{6} = \frac{1}{2}. \tag{5.6}$$

Now given that A has happened, what is the probability of B? In other words, what is the probability of getting a number divisible by 3 amongst the three numbers 2, 4 and 6? The answer is 1/3, so that

$$\text{Prob(B|A)} = \frac{1}{3}. \tag{5.7}$$

Substituting the results of expressions **5.6** and **5.7** in **5.5** gives

$$\frac{1}{2} \times \frac{1}{3} = \frac{1}{6},$$

which is clearly correct.

A more realistic example is the following. N psychiatrists interview a patient and are asked to say whether or not he is a schizophrenic. Of the N, r say he is; what is the probability that two of the psychiatrists chosen at random will both say that the patient is a schizophrenic? The probability that one psychiatrist (say A) chosen at random will classify the patient as a schizophrenic is $p_1 = r/N$. Now suppose that A does diagnose the patient as schizophrenic, then eliminate him from the sample of N. There are now $N-1$ psychiatrists left of whom $r-1$ say that the patient is schizophrenic. Next, choose another psychiatrist (B) at random from the $N-1$ psychiatrists. The probability that B will say the patient is schizophrenic, given that A has already said so, is $\mathrm{Prob}(B|A) = (r-1)/(N-1)$. Substituting these values in formula **5.5** we have

$$\mathrm{Prob}(A \ and \ B) = \mathrm{Prob}(A \times \mathrm{Prob}(B|A)$$

$$= \frac{r}{N} \times \frac{r-1}{N-1}$$

$$= \frac{r(r-1)}{N(N-1)}. \tag{5.8}$$

By a similar argument the probability that three psychiatrists drawn randomly from the sample of N will all say that the patient is schizophrenic is

$$\frac{r(r-1)(r-2)}{N(N-1)(N-2)}, \tag{5.9}$$

and so on.

To carry the discussion further, let us consider the following problem. It was concerned with the selection of patients (schizophrenics) for inclusion in a drug study. To ensure accuracy of diagnosis a number of psychiatrists were asked to co-operate. Now if only those patients which all psychiatrists diagnosed as schizophrenics were to be included in the investigation, a very large number of possible patients might have to be screened before an adequate sample would be obtained. On the other hand if patients were included in the study who were diagnosed as schizophrenics by *at least* two out of three psychiatrists, the required sample would be achieved more readily, and one would still have reasonable confidence in the accuracy of the diagnosis.

Suppose that r out of N psychiatrists say that a patient is schizophrenic and the remainder $N-r$ say he is not. Already we have found the probability, say $\mathrm{Prob}(AAA)$, that three psychiatrists chosen randomly from N give the desired result to be (expression **5.9**)

$$\text{Prob(AAA)} = \frac{r(r-1)(r-2)}{N(N-1)(N-2)}. \qquad \textbf{5.10}$$

By a similar argument,

$$\text{Prob(AAB)} = \frac{r(r-1)(N-r)}{N(N-1)(N-2)} \qquad \textbf{5.11}$$

is the probability that one, B, of three psychiatrists will say that the patient is not schizophrenic while the other two, AA, say he is. But the psychiatrist who says the patient is not schizophrenic may be any one of the three, hence the probability of AAB, or ABA, or BAA, is

$$\frac{3r(r-1)(N-r)}{N(N-1)(N-2)}. \qquad \textbf{5.12}$$

Adding together expressions **5.10** and **5.12** we find the probability that *at least* two out of three psychiatrists say the patient is schizophrenic to be

$$p_{2 \cdot 3} = \frac{r(r-1)(r-2) + 3r(r-1)(N-r)}{N(N-1)(N-2)}. \qquad \textbf{5.13}$$

6 Contingency Tables and Tests of Association

Introduction

In many observational studies the investigator is concerned not with continuous variables but with categories into one or other of which the individuals in his sample can be placed. Marital status is an example, and the categories involved might be somewhat as follows:

1. single,
2. married and living together,
3. married and living apart,
4. divorced,
5. widowed,
6. other living arrangements,
8. not known.

Other such variables are social class, occupation, country of origin, and so on. The categories decided upon for each variable should be exhaustive and mutually exclusive.

When members of a sample are classified simultaneously according to two such variables, then a rectangular display of frequencies occurs and the resulting table is known as a *contingency table*. Let us take an example. For a sample of 216 patients over forty-five years of age and suspected of having cerebral tumours, the presence (M) or absence $(\overline{M})$ of memory impairment was noted. After death autopsies were carried out and the sites of the tumours were identified. These were divided into four categories as follows:

I tumours of the anterior part of the cerebrum,
II tumours in the temporal lobes,
III deep-seated tumours around or in the third ventricle,
IV tumours associated with the tissue sheaths enclosing the cortex, and other tumours.

The results for the sample ($N = 216$) of patients were then placed in appropriate categories and are shown in Table 3 below.

Table 3
Sites of Tumours and Memory Impairment

		Sites				
		I	II	III	IV	Total
Memory	$\overline{M}$	17	18	15	36	86
Impairment	M	30(64)	10(36)	28(65)	62(63)	130
		47	28	43	98	216

Percentage impairment in brackets.

Given a contingency table such as Table 3, certain questions about the relative frequencies in the different cells might be asked. For example, we might inquire whether memory impairment is more closely associated with one site than another. To facilitate this comparison the percentage frequency of memory impairment for each site is entered in brackets in Table 3, and it is seen that whereas impairment was present over 60 per cent of the time with tumours in sites I, III and IV, it was present only 36 per cent of the time with tumours in site II. On this evidence one would tend to conclude that a patient who showed memory impairment, and who was suspected of having a cerebral tumour, was less likely to have that tumour in the temporal lobes than in one of the other sites in question. However, although the over-all sample is relatively large, the number of patients falling into each of the four sites is relatively small (only 28 for site II). In view of this one would like to have a method of assessing the probability that differences between the sites as great as those observed could have occurred by chance even if it were the case that memory impairment was equally likely to occur with tumours in any of the four sites. To answer this question a *chi-square* test can be employed. To do it we first calculate for each cell of the table the value we would expect to occur if there were no association between the symptom and the different sites of tumours. Let us call the expected value for the first cell in the table E_1, then, in the absence of association, we would expect

$$\frac{E_1}{47} = \frac{86}{216}$$

or $\quad E_1 = \dfrac{47 \times 86}{216} = 18 \cdot 7.$

By a similar argument we would expect the values E_2 and E_3 for cells two and three, to be respectively

$$E_2 = \frac{28 \times 86}{216} \quad \text{and} \quad E_3 = \frac{43 \times 86}{216}$$
$$= 11 \cdot 1 \qquad\qquad\qquad = 17 \cdot 1$$

We can now set up a table of expected frequencies as follows

18·7	11·1	17·1	E_4	86
E_5	E_6	E_7	E_8	130
47·0	28·0	43·0	98·0	216

From this table it is clear that

$E_5 = 47 - 18 \cdot 7 = 28 \cdot 3,$
$E_6 = 28 - 11 \cdot 1 = 16 \cdot 9, \qquad$ etc.

In other words once E_1, E_2 and E_3 have been found, the remaining expected frequencies can be obtained by deduction. The least number of expected values which has to be calculated before all the others can be deduced is known as the degrees of freedom (d.f.) for the table. This number can also be obtained by the formula

d.f. $= (c-1)(r-1),$

where the contingency table has c columns and r rows.
For each cell of the table we now calculate

$$\frac{(O-E)^2}{E}, \qquad\qquad\qquad \textbf{6.1}$$

where O is the observed frequency for that cell and E is the expected frequency on the null hypothesis. The sum of these quantities for all cells is the value of chi-square required, that is

$$\chi^2 = \Sigma \frac{(O-E)^2}{E}.$$

6.2

For the first cell

$$\frac{(O-E)^2}{E} = \frac{(17-18\cdot7)^2}{18\cdot7} = 0\cdot154.$$

Similar values were calculated for the other cells and they are

0·154	4·289	0·258	0·246
0·102	2·817	0·170	0·163.

The sum of these eight quantities is 8·2 and this is the value of χ^2 required. It is informative to note that it is made up primarily from the contributions for site II. The quantity $\chi^2 = 8\cdot2$ is now referred to the chi-square distribution (Appendix 3) with 3 degrees of freedom. There it is found (row 3 column 2) that a value of 7·81 would occur by chance 5 per cent of the time even if there were no association between the two methods of classification. But since the value we obtained, namely 8·2, is greater than 7·81, our result is significant beyond the 5 per cent level, in other words it would be expected to occur by chance less than once in twenty times. Since this is a relatively rare occurrence, we conclude that there is evidence of a real association between site and type of tumour. Examination of the percentages in Table 3 strongly suggests that the significant result obtained is due to the relatively small percentage of patients with tumours in site II who have memory impairment. In other words tumours in the temporal lobes are less likely to lead to memory impairment than tumours in the other sites considered.

Fourfold Tables

The chi-square test can be applied to a contingency table of any size. Many refinements of the test exist which enable one, in certain circumstances, to partition the over-all χ^2 value into independent components and thus to test more specific hypotheses about the data than the test just described provides. As the author has summarized these procedures elsewhere (Maxwell, 1961), they will not be discussed here, but in this elementary account it is desirable to mention in more detail the simplest case of all.

The simplest test of association occurs when the table is fourfold and the calculations can then be performed by use of a simple formula. Let the observed frequencies be denoted by the letters a to d, as shown below

a	b	$a+b$
c	d	$c+d$
$a+c$	$b+d$	N

Then the chi-square is given by the formula

$$\chi^2 = \frac{N(ad-bc)^2}{(a+b)(c+d)(a+c)(b+d)} \qquad 6.3$$

with one degree of freedom. This formula gives exactly the same result as formula **6.2** when applied to a fourfold table. Moreover, if the sample size N is small (say $N < 40$), a correction term can be included in the formula to give a more accurate test of significance. The formula now becomes

$$\chi^2 = \frac{N(|ad-bc| - \tfrac{1}{2}N)^2}{(a+b)(c+d)(a+c)(b+d)}, \qquad 6.4$$

where the vertical lines either side of $ad-bc$ mean that the value of this expression is to be taken as positive whether its algebraic value is positive or negative.

Let us take an example. In an investigation of a sample of 20 epileptic children by E.E.G., the occurrence of cerebral lesions in the anterior and posterior regions of the right and left hemispheres was noted and the following results obtained

	Right	Left	
Anterior	3(a)	8(b)	11
Posterior	7(c)	2(d)	9
	10	10	20

Do these data supply evidence of an association between hemisphere and site of lesion?

Applying formula **6.4** we obtain the value

$$\chi^2 = \frac{20(|6-56|-10)^2}{11 \times 9 \times 10 \times 10}$$

$$= \frac{20 \times 40^2}{9900}$$

$$= 3.23.$$

Referring to the tables, with one degree of freedom, we find the 5 per cent value to be 3.84, and since our value is only 3.23, we have insufficient evidence to reject the null hypothesis at this level of significance, or to claim an association between hemisphere and site of lesion. Nevertheless, the data taken at their face value strongly suggest that posterior lesions tend to occur more frequently in the right hemisphere and anterior lesions in the left. To confirm this contention, if in fact it is true, more data would be required. If in repeat experiments results similar to those already obtained were found, then the contention that an association did in fact exist would be supported, and the results might safely be combined in an over-all test (see Maxwell, 1961, Chapter V). But if they were consistently dissimilar, we would be wise to conclude that the original set of data were atypical.

Another method of procedure is as follows. We might, on the basis of our first set of results or in the light of other prior knowledge, feel justified in setting up a 'one-tail' hypothesis to the effect that posterior lesions were more frequent in the right hemisphere than in the left. The experiment could then be repeated and a result which was significant at the 10 per cent level would supply the confirmation required. This simple test unfortunately is somewhat approximate unless the lateral frequencies in the fourfold table are equal, or nearly so. But by a more elaborate calculation, the exact probability for the one-tail test can be found (Maxwell, 1961, p. 23); the result can also be read off directly from published tables (see Finney, 1963).

7 Correlation and Regression

Introduction

In the behavioural sciences, especially in psychology, methods of correlation and regression are extensively used. This is due in part to the fact that they were amongst the first statistical tools made available to psychologists, having been introduced by Galton before the beginning of the present century. But there is another reason for their popularity. It is relatively easy in studies of human reaction and behaviour to obtain measures for each member of a sample of subjects on each of a number of variables – age, height, weight and other physical measurements; socio-economic status; I.Q., educational attainments, etc.; not to mention physiological variables such as muscle tension, galvanic skin response; and psychiatric variables such as ratings on neuroticism, extraversion, depression, and so on. Now measurements on variables such as these tend to be related to a greater or lesser extent and it is natural to seek a way of measuring such relationships, or of predicting for a given value of one variable the probable value of another. To a first approximation the correlation coefficient provides an answer to the first problem while a regression equation provides an answer to the second.

Over the years several coefficients for measuring the co-variability or correlation between a pair of concomitant variables have been suggested. For continuous variables, such as age, I.Q., etc., the most commonly used is the *product moment correlation coefficient*. The procedure by which it is obtained is relatively straightforward and an example is given below.

The I.Q.s for a random sample of 9 feeble-minded patients (though in practice a much larger sample would be required) in the age range twenty-one to thirty years inclusive, as ascertained by two tests, the Stanford–Binet (X') and the Wechsler–Bellevue (Y'), were

	Patient									
	1	2	3	4	5	6	7	8	9	*Mean*
X'	80	65	51	67	72	68	64	91	71	69·9
Y'	82	77	58	66	75	81	72	99	72	75·8

The mean score on variable Y' is seen to be 5·9 points of I.Q. greater than the mean score on X', and hence the two tests are not strictly comparable as regards the magnitudes of the actual scores. But a correlation coefficient is not concerned with magnitude *per se*: it is a measure of concomitant variation and tells us whether high scores on one variable tend to go with high scores on the other variable and vice versa (i.e. positive correlation), or whether high scores on one tend to go with low scores on the other and vice versa (i.e. negative correlation), or whether no such tendencies exist (zero correlation). Indeed, a correlation coefficient can be shown to be independent of the means of the scores on the two variables and can be calculated for pairs of measurements which have entirely different metrics, such as height and weight.

The scores given above are numerically large and so somewhat awkward to deal with, but since a correlation coefficient is independent of the means of the variables the scores can be simplified by subtracting a constant from each set. If we replace X' by $X = X' - 60$, say, and Y' by $Y = Y' - 70$, we get the smaller numbers, given in columns 2 and 3 of Table 4 below, which are easier to handle.

Table 4   Calculations for Product Moment Correlation

| 1 | 2 | 3 | 4 | 5 | 6 |
Patient	X	Y	X^2	Y^2	XY
1	20	12	400	144	240
2	5	7	25	49	35
3	−9	−12	81	144	108
4	7	−4	49	16	−28
5	12	5	144	25	60
6	8	11	64	121	88
7	4	2	16	4	8
8	31	29	961	841	899
9	11	2	121	4	22
	89	52	1861	1348	1432

The calculation shown in Table 4 is now performed and the total of each column obtained. If a desk calculating machine is available these calculations can be carried out with speed and accuracy and only the totals need be recorded. To obtain the correlation coefficient we require the sum of squares of the deviations of the X-scores from their mean $\bar{X}$, namely

$$\sum x^2 = \sum (X - \bar{X})^2$$
$$= \sum X^2 - \frac{(\sum X)^2}{N} \qquad \qquad \textbf{7.1}$$
$$= 1861 - \frac{89^2}{9}$$
$$= 980 \cdot 9.$$

We require a similar quantity for the Y-scores, namely

$$\sum y^2 = \sum (Y - \bar{Y})^2 \qquad \qquad \textbf{7.2}$$
$$= \sum Y^2 - \frac{(\sum Y)^2}{N}$$
$$= 1348 - \frac{52^2}{9}$$
$$= 1047 \cdot 6.$$

We also require the sum of products of the deviations of X and Y scores from their respective means, namely

$$\sum xy = \sum (X - \bar{X})(Y - \bar{Y})$$
$$= \sum XY - \frac{\sum X \sum Y}{N} \qquad \qquad \textbf{7.3}$$
$$= 1432 - \frac{89 \times 52}{9}$$
$$= 917 \cdot 8.$$

Now if the product moment correlation between the two variables in the population of feeble-minded patients in the given age-range is denoted by the Greek letter ρ (rho), an estimate r of ρ obtained from a random sample is given by the formula

$$r = \frac{\sum xy}{\sqrt{(\sum x^2 \sum y^2)}}. \qquad \qquad 7.4$$

For our data we then find

$$r = \frac{917 \cdot 8}{\sqrt{980 \cdot 9} \times \sqrt{1047 \cdot 6}}$$
$$= \frac{917 \cdot 8}{31 \cdot 32 \times 32 \cdot 37}$$
$$= 0 \cdot 905.$$

By a little algebra it can be shown that the formula for the correlation coefficient can also be written in the form

$$\rho = \frac{1 \sum xy}{N\sigma_x \sigma_y}, \qquad \qquad 7.5$$

so that ρ is the average of the sum of products of N pairs of standardized scores, x/σ_x and y/σ_y. Standardized scores have means of zero and standard deviations of unity; ρ will have a value equal to, or lying between, $+1$ and -1. A value $\rho = +1$ corresponds to the case where there is perfect positive concomitant agreement between the pairs of scores, and $\rho = -1$ to the case where there is perfect inverse (negative) agreement. The correlation of $0 \cdot 905$ just found between I.Q. scores on the Stanford–Binet and Wechsler tests is close to unity, hence we can conclude that (even though one test has a higher mean than the other) the patients, if ranked on the basis of their scores on the tests, would have rankings which were in close agreement.

Interpreting a Correlation Coefficient

We have seen that a correlation coefficient is a measure of concomitant agreement between pairs of scores on two variables, and if its numerical value differs from zero (a significance test will be discussed later), it is customary to say that the two variables are themselves correlated. But the coefficient itself is just an index of agreement and on its own supplies no information about the reasons why the variables are related. This question can only be answered from prior knowledge of the nature of the variables themselves. In the case of the two intelligence tests, Stanford–Binet and Wechsler–Bellevue, the explanation of the positive correlation of 0·905 is relatively straightforward for the items comprising both tests are concerned with problems of reasoning and comprehension. But let us consider another less obvious example. For certain areas in London a correlation of $-0·92$ was found between the two variables X and Y where X is the proportion of the area which consisted of open spaces, and Y is the proportion of accidents which were accidents to children. At its face value we might conclude that this strong inverse relationship indicated a possible way of preventing accidents, namely by providing each district in the city with a liberal supply of open spaces. But a closer look at the data suggests that this is not the full story. For instance Hampstead and Westminster are two areas in which the provision of open spaces is liberal and the numbers of accidents to children are relatively low, but these areas are also high-class residential areas in which families tend to be relatively small and nursemaids relatively numerous. Hence these factors, in addition to 'open spaces' may contribute to the high value of the coefficient obtained. No doubt further inquiry would reveal other factors which played a part.

Occasionally, of course, correlations are found for which it is difficult to give any rational explanation at all. The late Professor Udny Yule, for instance, reported a significant correlation between the number of apples imported into Great Britain and the number of divorces on each of a series of years: his example provides a salutary warning not to identify 'correlation' and 'causation'.

In some cases the explanation of an obtained correlation between two variables, which are ostensibly independent, may arise because each is correlated with a third variable. For instance scores on a test of general knowledge might be found to correlate highly with children's height if children from a wide age-range were concerned, the correlation being due largely to the relationship between age and height rather than between general knowledge and height. Occasionally too 'spurious correlations' are reported. Professor J. Neyman once gave a hypothetical example to show how such a correlation might arise. Suppose that for each of N different counties the following 'counts' were obtained

S number of storks,
B number of babies,
W number of women of child-bearing age.

If from these data we generate the two variables

$\qquad X =$ density of storks (per woman),
and $\qquad Y =$ birth rate,

then X and Y would tend to be correlated, with the implication that storks may indeed bring babies. The fallacy lies in the fact that X and Y depend on a common argument W. If, for a given area, W tends to be large relative to S and to B, then for that area both X and Y will tend to be small. The converse will also be true, and the outcome will be a tendency for the correlation between X and Y to be large. Here it is worth mentioning that the spurious factor in the correlation can be eradicated by using a partial correlation coefficient, but the matter will not be discussed further here (see McNemar, 1962).

Other Indices of Correlation

Apart from the product moment correlation coefficient, which is universally used with continuous data, several other indices of agreement are in common use. One of these is the *rank correlation coefficient* which is employed when actual scores for the subjects in the sample are not available but it is possible to rank them with regard to two or more variables. Methods whereby rank correlations can be calculated are described in most textbooks on elementary statistics and details will not be given here.

Frequently, too, one requires a measure of correlation between dichotomously scored variables, and coefficients such as the tetrachoric correlation coefficient (McNemar, 1962) or the fourfold point (also called the Phi) correlation coefficient are then commonly used. The latter is simply the product moment correlation between two variables for which the only admissible scores are 0 and 1. These might be the scores allocated to items in an intelligence test which were scored 0 if the subject gave an incorrect answer and 1 if he gave a correct answer. A similar scoring system might be used for questions in a questionnaire to which the subject was asked to answer either 'No' or 'Yes', or 'Disagree' or 'Agree'. Suppose that for two items in an intelligence test, the scores for N subjects are summarized as follows

		Item I		
		0	*1*	
Item J	1	a	b	$a+b$
	0	c	d	$c+d$
		$a+c$	$b+d$	N

This is the situation in which b of the N subjects get both items correct and c get both incorrect; a get the first item incorrect and the second correct, while d get the reverse. The fourfold point correlation between the items is then given by the formula

$$r = \frac{bc - ad}{\sqrt{\{(a+b)(c+d)(a+c)(b+d)\}}}. \qquad 7.6$$

This formula can be used with confidence when the proportion of children getting either item correct lies in the range $0 \cdot 2$ to $0 \cdot 8$.

Formula 7.6 might also be used to find a measure of agreement between two psychiatrists who had rated a number of patients regarding the presence or absence of certain symptoms. For instance two psychiatrists interviewed 66 patients and their findings for the symptom 'impairment of memory' were as follows

		Second psychiatrist		
		Absent	*Present*	*Total*
First	*Present*	13(a)	4(b)	17
psychiatrist	*Absent*	48(c)	1(d)	49
	Total	61	5	66

Applying formula 7.6 to these results we find the correlation or coefficient of agreement between the two psychiatrists to be 0·355.

These data, however, require further scrutiny. In the first instance we notice that not only does the symptom occur relatively infrequently but also that whereas one psychiatrist reports it present in 17 of the 66 patients, the other does so in only 5 instances. It is thus clear that an adequate comparison between the two psychiatrists is not provided by the coefficient of agreement given above; some assessment of the bias between them is also needed.

We might thus inquire whether the bias observed is such as might occur relatively frequently by chance or whether it is indicative of a real difference between the psychiatrists. This can be assessed by testing whether the two (correlated) proportions $17/66 = 0.2576$ and $5/66 = 0.0758$ differ significantly. The test can be done by applying the formula (see Maxwell, 1961, p. 27)

$$z = \frac{|a-d|-1}{\sqrt{(a+d)}};\qquad\qquad 7.7$$

the result is then referred to the normal distribution. In formula 7.7 the vertical lines either side of a–d indicate that we take the value to be positive whether it turns out to be positive or negative. For the data in question

$$z = \frac{|13-1|-1}{\sqrt{(13+1)}} = \frac{11}{3.74} = 2.94,$$

so that the difference observed would occur by chance very infrequently indeed. The 1 per cent value is $z = 2.58$, hence we conclude that there is a real difference between the two psychiatrists regarding their diagnosis of the symptom 'impairment of memory'. This finding, together with the fact that in the opinion of the second psychiatrist the incidence of the symptom occurs in a proportion of only 0·076 of the patients throws doubt on the value (0·355) of the coefficient of agreement given by the fourfold point correlation coefficient.

In situations such as this a preferable measure of agreement is provided by a coefficient called the *kappa coefficient* (κ). Using the same symbols as before, kappa is given by

$$\kappa = \frac{2\,(bc-ad)}{(c+d)(b+d)+(a+b)(a+c)}. \qquad \textbf{7.8}$$

This formula is the ratio of the two quantities, (i) the difference between the observed proportion of agreements (p_o) and the expected proportion (p_c) due to chance, where

$$p_o = \frac{b+c}{N} \qquad \textbf{7.9}$$

and $\quad p_c = \dfrac{(a+b)(b+d)+(a+c)(c+d)}{N^2}, \qquad \textbf{7.10}$

and (ii) and the quantity $1-p_c$, which is the expected proportion of agreements not due to chance,

i.e. $\quad \kappa = \dfrac{p_o-p_c}{1-p_c}.$

On substituting the observed values in the formula **7.8** we find $\kappa = 0\cdot279$, which is considerably less than the value, $r = 0\cdot355$, given by formula **7.6**.

The variance of κ is estimated approximately by the formula

$$\text{var}\,(\kappa) = \frac{1}{(1-p_c)^2}\,\frac{p_o(1-p_o)}{N} \qquad \textbf{7.11}$$

(see Everitt, 1968).

Significance of a Correlation Coefficient

Even if the true correlation between two variables in the population were zero, one would not expect to get an answer of exactly zero when estimating the correlation from a sample of subjects drawn randomly from that population. Hence it is necessary to have a method of finding the probability that an obtained correlation did indeed come from a population in which the true correlation between the two variables in question is zero. There are several methods of answering this problem but one which is valid even for relatively small samples (say $N < 30$) is to calculate the statistic

$$t = \frac{r\sqrt{(N-2)}}{\sqrt{(1-r^2)}}, \qquad\qquad 7.12$$

where r is the estimated value of ρ and N is the sample size, and to refer the obtained value of t to the t-distribution with $N-2$ degrees of freedom. For example if for two variates X and Y, $N = 17$ and $r = 0.5$, then

$$t = \frac{0.5\sqrt{15}}{\sqrt{0.75}} = \frac{0.5 \times 3.873}{0.866} = 2.24.$$

With $N-2 = 15$ degrees of freedom we see from Appendix 2 that $t = 2.13$ at the 5 per cent level. Since our value of t is 2·24 and so is greater than 2·13, a value of $r = 0.5$ would occur by chance less than once in 20 times (5 per cent level of significance). Since this would be a relatively rare occurrence, we conclude that the true correlation between X and Y is unlikely to be zero. The best estimate of ρ that we have is the value $r = 0.5$ obtained from our data.

Tables are available which give, for different values of N, the size r must be to be significantly different from zero at different levels of significance. When either the tables or formula **7.12** are used, certain assumptions about the data are made. The most important of these is that the variables X and Y are normally distributed in the population, but in practice it is wise to make a scattergram of the scores to ensure that the relationship between them is elliptical or circular in shape since normality of the variables taken separately does not necessarily imply this.

Linear Regression

The term *regression* was introduced into statistics by Galton, when comparing characteristics of parents with those of their children. In the case of height, for example, he found that while the mean height of adult sons of tall fathers was less than the mean of the fathers themselves, the mean height of sons of short fathers was greater than that of the fathers themselves.

In other words for fathers of a given height the mean of their sons always 'regressed' towards the overall mean of all sons (or, for that matter, of all fathers since the two tended to be equal). This phenomenon occurs because of the lack of perfect correlation, whatever the cause, between the heights of fathers and sons. But it is true only on the average and need not be true in the case of any individual son.

Despite its rather confusing origin the word 'regression' (or regression line) is now widely used to indicate a trend in the value of one measure as some other related measure is allowed to vary. The idea is most easily understood by means of an example. In Table 5 two measures, X and Y, for each of a sample of 17 people are given. X is the person's age in years, while Y is the rate of flow of blood plasma through his kidneys (measured in millilitres per minute per 1·73 square metres of body surface area – though these details need not concern us unduly).

Table 5
Rate (Y) of Flow of Blood in the Kidney for Individuals of X Years of Age

Individual	X	Y
1	40	467
2	40	550
3	40	573
4	45	430
5	45	470
6	45	476
7	45	520
8	50	466
9	50	430
10	50	375
11	55	352
12	55	406
13	55	426
14	55	441
15	60	340
16	60	373
17	60	405
Mean	50	441·2

These data are plotted in Figure 7 and it is immediately obvious that the rate of flow of blood decreases with age (indeed for a sample of 51 cases the correlation between the two variables was found to be -0.856). If we wished to use these data to estimate the rate of blood-flow for a person of given age we could fit a line through the data from which estimates could be obtained. Following accepted nomenclature the line would be called the regression line of Y on X, that is the line for estimating Y for a given value of X.

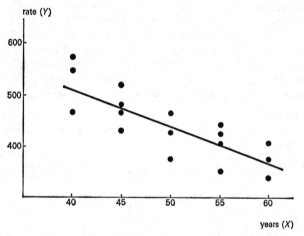

Figure 7 Rate of flow of blood in the kidney at different ages.

The line could be fitted by eye, but if greater precision were desirable mathematical formulae are available for finding the algebraic equation of the line of 'best fit'. The 'best fit' (or 'least square') line is a line such that the sum of the squares of the distances (parallel to the Y-axis) of all the points from it is a minimum. Indeed the calculations for finding the slope of the line are similar to those given when discussing correlation. We require Σx^2 and Σxy and the slope b of the line is then estimated by the expression

$$b = \frac{\Sigma xy}{\Sigma x^2}.$$ **7.13**

For the above data $b = -7.6$, which means that for every year of increase in age the rate of blood-flow, on the average, decreases by 7·6 points. It can be shown also that this line passes through the point in the figure corresponding to the means of the variates (namely $\overline{X} = 50$, $\overline{Y} = 441$); hence its position is completely defined. Methods also exist for testing whether the assumption is tenable that a straight line gives an adequate fit to the data. One can also test whether the slope of the line differs significantly from the horizontal, that is whether the population value, β (beta) of b, is zero; in straightforward cases the test is equivalent to testing whether the correlation coefficient between the two variates differs from zero.

8 Simple Tests of Significance

Introduction

It is widely felt that psychologists and other behavioural scientists tend to over-emphasize the role of tests of significance in experimental work to the neglect of problems of estimation such as are discussed in chapter 4. To some extent the criticism is justified, but over-emphasis is largely a reflection of the nature of much of the data in question. Measurements of psychological phenomena, as noted earlier, tend to be imprecise and it is frequently the case that variation is considerable not only from subject to subject but for a single subject on different occasions. In view of this variation it is difficult to assess at a glance the performance of subjects on different occasions and in different experimental situations, whereas a test of significance, which takes the amount of variability in the data into account, provides a useful quantitative appraisal of the results. Perhaps the most important warning to the amateur is not to take the word 'significance' too literally. A difference between the mean scores of two samples of patients, which is 'significant' in the probability or statistical sense, may still not be of sufficient magnitude to be of any great importance in a clinical sense. In this chapter some simple tests for comparing pairs of means will be described and the distinction between statistical and clinical significance will be emphasized.

Standard Error of the Difference between Two Means

Let us consider a situation in which N patients in a random sample from some population, where N is relatively large, say 100 or more, each do the Wechsler–Bellevue Test (X) and

Raven's Matrices Test (Y) so that we have N pairs of scores (X_i, Y_i), where i stands for the ith patient ($i = 1, 2,\ldots, N$). In practice one would normally work with the observed scores, but to simplify the algebra we will assume that each X-score has the mean of all the X-scores subtracted from it and each Y-score has the mean of the Y-scores subtracted from it, so that we have in fact N pairs of deviational scores (x_i, y_i). These could be arranged as follows

Subjects					
1	2	3	4	...	N
Test X x_1	x_2	x_3	x_4	...	x_N
Test Y y_1	y_2	y_3	y_4	...	y_N

Since the scores are paired, the difference

$$d_i = x_i - y_i$$

between each pair could be taken and the variance of the differences, $V(d)$, estimated in the usual way, namely,

$$V(d) = s^2 = \frac{\sum d_i^2}{N-1}. \qquad \textbf{8.1}$$

By expression **4.2** the standard error of the mean difference, $\bar{D} = \bar{X} - \bar{Y}$, is then given by $s/\sqrt{N}$. But it is informative to derive this standard error directly from the x- and y-scores, for this procedure shows explicitly how possible correlation between the two sets of scores is taken into account.

If the differences are squared and summed we obtain

$$\sum d_i^2 = \sum (x_i - y_i)^2$$
$$= \sum x_i^2 + \sum y_i^2 - 2 \sum x_i y_i. \qquad \textbf{8.2}$$

Using expression **7.4** this equation can be expressed in the form

$$\sum d_i^2 = \sum x_i^2 + \sum y_i^2 - 2r\sqrt{(\sum x_i^2 \sum y_i^2)},$$

which, on dividing by $N-1$, gives

$$V(d) = s_x^2 + s_y^2 - 2rs_x s_y, \qquad \textbf{8.3}$$

where s_x^2 and s_y^2 are the estimates of the variance of the variables X and Y, and s_x and s_y are the corresponding standard deviations. Hence, by analogy with formula **4.1** an estimate of the error variance of the difference between the means of the scores on the two tests is given by

$$\frac{1}{N}(s_x^2 + s_y^2 - 2rs_x s_y), \qquad \textbf{8.4}$$

which numerically is equal to $V(d)/N$. The standard error of the difference is the square root of expression **8.4**.

For the two mental tests in question the results for a sample of 180 patients were

$\overline{X} = 82.90;$ $\overline{Y} = 83.98;$ $s_x = 11.08;$
$s_y = 9.98;$ $r = 0.79.$

On substituting the relevant values in expression **8.4** we find the error variance of the difference between $\overline{X}$ and $\overline{Y}$ to be

$$\frac{122.77 + 99.60 - 2 \times 0.79 \times 11.08 \times 9.98}{180} = \frac{47.66}{180}$$
$$= 0.265.$$

Hence the standard error of the difference between the two means is

$\sqrt{0.265} = 0.515.$

In other words if we had drawn many random samples of size 180 from the population of patients in question and for each sample had found the mean difference $\overline{D}$, where $\overline{D} = \overline{X} - \overline{Y}$ these values of $\overline{D}$ would have a distribution with standard deviation (standard error) of approximately 0.515.

The value 0.515 can now be used for setting up confidence intervals for the mean difference

$\overline{Y} - \overline{X} = (83.98 - 82.90) = 1.08.$

The 95 per cent confidence intervals are

$1.08 \pm 1.96 \times 0.515,$

namely 2.09 and 0.07. Hence if we say that the true difference between the means of the two tests lies between 2.09 and 0.07, there is a 0.95 probability that we are right, in the sense that in making this judgement in a large number of identical but independent cases we would be right 95 times in 100.

Testing the significance of the difference between two means for correlated data (large samples)

To test the significance of the difference between the two means in the last example we set up the null hypothesis that the true mean difference of the intelligence tests in the population from which the sample is drawn is zero. The difference obtained is then expressed in standardized form as follows

$$z = \frac{\overline{Y} - \overline{X}}{\text{standard error of difference}} \qquad 8.5$$

$$= \frac{83 \cdot 98 - 82 \cdot 90}{0 \cdot 515}$$

$$= 2 \cdot 10$$

and the answer is referred to the normal distribution. Since the value $z = 1 \cdot 96$ cuts off tails of the distribution each equal to $0 \cdot 025$ of the total area, these tails represent the rejection area at the 5 per cent level for the null hypothesis that the two means do not differ. The obtained value of $z = 2 \cdot 10$ is greater than $1 \cdot 96$ and hence lies in the rejection area, so we may reject the null hypothesis and say that we have evidence beyond the 5 per cent level of significance that the two means differ. In other words the difference obtained would be expected to occur by chance less than once in twenty times on average in repeated sampling.

But it is essential to remember that though a difference between two means may be found to be significant in the probability sense, the difference itself may not be sufficiently large to be of any great practical consequence. For the two tests just considered the 95 per cent confidence limits of the difference were shown to be $2 \cdot 09$ and $0 \cdot 07$, which is roughly 2 points of I.Q. For practical purposes it would thus appear that the two tests give roughly equivalent results as regards their means. However, the correlation of $0 \cdot 79$ between the two tests is well below $1 \cdot 00$, indicating that the scores obtained by individual subjects vary to a considerable degree. In addition the tests are not identical as regards psychological content, so that when assessing a patient's I.Q. it would be desirable, if time permitted, to administer both tests and perhaps average the results obtained.

Since the difference between the mean scores on the two tests is so small, one may ask whether the test of significance was worth doing. Indeed the 'significant' result in this instance is almost an embarrassment. But in defence of tests of significance another aspect of the problem is worth considering. Suppose that prior to collecting the data it was decided that a difference of 6 points of I.Q. between the means would be considered of clinical importance, then it would still be necessary having obtained such a difference to check how frequently, on the null hypothesis, it might arise in repeated sampling. In other words the variability between subjects' scores might be so great that a difference of even 6 points between the means might occur so frequently that the initial decision about its importance would require reconsideration. A test of significance is a valuable method of checking this point.

Comparing Means Obtained from Two Independent Samples

In the last example there were two scores for each subject in the sample so that it was possible to calculate the correlation coefficient between the scores on the two tests. It was also shown how this coefficient entered into the estimate of the standard error of the difference between the means. But frequently we wish to test whether the mean scores on a single variable for two independent samples of subjects differ. Since the samples are independent and the scores cannot be matched in pairs, the possibility of their being correlated is ruled out.

Consider again the data from a survey of London schoolchildren, in which the variable being measured was weight in kilograms. There was a sample of 336 children from one-child families and a sample of 72 children from families of five or more children. The data were as follows:

Size of family	N	Mean weight	S.D.
1 child	336	37·01	6·60
5 children or more	72	32·47	6·62

The problem is to test whether these two samples are drawn from one and the same population or whether there are two distinct populations where weight is concerned.

The error variance of the means using the square of expression **4.1** are respectively

$$\frac{6 \cdot 60^2}{336} \quad \text{and} \quad \frac{6 \cdot 62^2}{72},$$

so that, by analogy with expression **8.4**, the error variance of the difference between the means is

$$\frac{6 \cdot 60^2}{336} + \frac{6 \cdot 62^2}{72} = 0 \cdot 7383$$

and the standard error is $\sqrt{0 \cdot 7383} = 0 \cdot 8592$; the term involving r in expression **8.4** disappears since the samples are independent. The difference between the two means, namely $37 \cdot 01 - 32 \cdot 47 = 4 \cdot 54$, can now be expressed in standardized form, giving

$$z = \frac{4 \cdot 54}{0 \cdot 8592} = 5 \cdot 28.$$

This value, when referred to the normal distribution, is found to lie very far out in the tail and would occur by chance very infrequently ($P < 0 \cdot 001$); hence we conclude that the samples of children are drawn from populations with different mean weights. Children of eleven years of age from families of five or more children on the average weigh less than children of the same age from one-child families. The words 'on the average' should be noted for a percentage of the children from the larger families may well have weights above the mean of the children from one-child families. Indeed this percentage can be estimated. What is required is the percentage of children in a population with mean weight $32 \cdot 47$ and standard deviation $6 \cdot 62$ whose weights are greater than $37 \cdot 01$. Here the z-value is

$$z = \frac{37 \cdot 01 - 32 \cdot 47}{6 \cdot 62}$$

$$= 0 \cdot 69.$$

On referring this value to the tables of the normal distribution it is found to correspond to a proportion of the total area under the curve equal to $0 \cdot 7549$, hence the proportion of the curve above $0 \cdot 69$ standard deviations is $1 - 0 \cdot 7549 = 0 \cdot 2451$ or $24 \cdot 5$

per cent. Consequently we would expect 24·5 per cent of children from the larger family sizes to have weights above the average for one-child families.

Written in symbols the formula for comparing the means of two independent samples is

$$z = \frac{\bar{X}_1 - \bar{X}_2}{\sqrt{(\sigma_1^2/n_1 + \sigma_2^2/n_2)}}, \qquad 8.6$$

where $\bar{X}_1$ and $\bar{X}_2$ are the means of the two samples, σ_1 and σ_2 their standard deviations and n_1 and n_2 their sample sizes respectively. Generally σ_1 and σ_2 are not known and have to be replaced by their estimates s_1 and s_2 obtained from the data.

Small Sample Theory

It was noted in chapter 4 that when the sample size is small and when the standard deviation is unknown and has to be estimated from the data, the expression

$$t = \frac{\bar{X} - \mu}{s/\sqrt{N}} \qquad 8.7$$

is not normally distributed but depends on the number of degrees of freedom on which s is based. This fact has to be taken into account when comparing means of small samples (say N less than about 60).

In an experiment involving depressed patients the amount of saliva (measured in grammes) was noted every two hours over a 24-hour period. For a sample of 4 patients the weights (M) at 6.00 a.m. and (A) at 2.00 p.m. respectively were as follows:

Patient	6.00 a.m. (M)	2.00 p.m. (A)	Difference (D)
1	1·484	0·857	0·627
2	1·971	1·064	0·907
3	1·753	0·905	0·848
4	1·408	0·884	0·524
Total	6·616	3·710	2·906
Mean	1·6540	0·9275	0·7265

The problem here is to test whether the two samples of observations are drawn from populations in which the true means are equal. Since the observations are paired, their differences may be considered and the problem now becomes one of testing the hypothesis that the true mean of the difference is zero. The first step is to find an estimate, s, of the standard deviation of the differences.

$$\Sigma \, D^2 = 0{\cdot}627^2 + 0{\cdot}907^2 + \ldots = 2{\cdot}2095;$$

hence Σd^2, the sum of squares of the deviations of the differences from their mean, is

$$
\begin{aligned}
\Sigma \, d^2 &= \Sigma \, (D - \bar{D})^2 \\
&= \Sigma \, D^2 - \frac{(\Sigma \, D)^2}{n} \\
&= 2{\cdot}2905 - \frac{2{\cdot}906^2}{4} \\
&= 0{\cdot}0983,
\end{aligned}
$$

and
$$
\begin{aligned}
s^2 &= \frac{\Sigma \, d^2}{n-1} \\
&= \frac{0{\cdot}0983}{3} \\
&= 0{\cdot}0328.
\end{aligned}
$$

The standard deviation of the difference thus is

$$s = \sqrt{0{\cdot}0328} = 0{\cdot}181.$$

Using expression **8.7** we now have

$$
\begin{aligned}
t &= \frac{0{\cdot}7265}{0{\cdot}181/2} \\
&= 8{\cdot}03,
\end{aligned}
$$

with $n-1 = 3$ degrees of freedom.

When this result is referred to the t-distribution (Appendix 2, row 3) it is found to be significant beyond the 1 per cent level, hence we may safely conclude that mean saliva weights at 6.00 a.m. are different from those at 2.00 p.m.

t-Tests for Independent Samples

A natural extension of the *t*-test allows the means for two independent samples (which need not have an equal number of observations in each) to be compared. In the investigation just mentioned a sample of normal control subjects also had their saliva weights measured and the scores (in grammes) for 5 patients and 4 controls at 9.00 p.m. were as follows:

	Patients X	Controls Y
	0·162	0·391
	0·203	0·497
	0·171	0·478
	0·151	0·384
	0·167	
Total	0·854	1·750
	$\overline{X} = 0{\cdot}171$	$\overline{Y} = 0{\cdot}438$

On the assumption that the variation in the two populations from which the samples are drawn are equal, a pooled estimate of the variance can be obtained by the expression

$$s^2 = \frac{\Sigma\,x^2 + \Sigma\,y^2}{n_1 + n_2 - 2}, \qquad\qquad 8.8$$

where $\Sigma\,x^2 = \Sigma\,X^2 - \dfrac{(\Sigma\,X)^2}{n_1}$

and $\Sigma\,y^2 = \Sigma\,Y^2 - \dfrac{(\Sigma\,Y)^2}{n_2}$,

n_1 and n_2 being the sizes of the respective samples. For the data concerned

$$\Sigma\,X^2 = 0{\cdot}1474,$$

hence $\Sigma\,x^2 = 0{\cdot}1474 - \dfrac{0{\cdot}854^2}{5}$

$$= 0{\cdot}001521,$$

$$\Sigma\,Y^2 = 0{\cdot}7758,$$

and $\Sigma\,y^2 = 0{\cdot}7758 - \dfrac{1{\cdot}750^2}{4}$

$$= 0{\cdot}010205.$$

Substituting these values (and $n_1 = 5$ and $n_2 = 4$) in expression **8.8** gives

$s^2 = 0.001675$.

The standard error of $\bar{D}$, the difference between $\bar{X}$ and $\bar{Y}$, is now estimated by

$$\sqrt{\left[s^2\left(\frac{1}{n_1}+\frac{1}{n_2}\right)\right]} = \sqrt{[0.001675(\tfrac{1}{5}+\tfrac{1}{4})]}$$
$$= 0.027455. \qquad\qquad \textbf{8.9}$$

The *t*-test is

$$t = \frac{\bar{Y}-\bar{X}}{\text{standard error of the difference}}$$
$$= \frac{0.438-0.171}{0.027455}$$
$$= 9.72.$$

Since the estimate of s is based on $n_1 + n_2 - 2 = 7$ degrees of freedom, the value $t = 9.72$ is referred to row 7 of the table (Appendix 2) and the result is found to be significant beyond the 0.1 per cent level. Consequently, it is safe to conclude that the mean saliva score for controls is greater than that for patients.

Since the means for the two groups differ by such a large margin and the standard deviations are relatively small, it would appear that the saliva test could usefully be used to distinguish between patients and controls. Using the mean of 0.171 as an estimate of the population mean for patients, we would expect 95 per cent of the population of patients to have saliva weights lying within the limits –

$0.171 \pm 2.36 \times \sqrt{0.001675}$, namely 0.268 and 0.084,

where 2.36 is obtained from the *t*-distribution at the 5 per cent level under 7 degrees of freedom. Similar limits for the control group are

$0.438 \pm 2.36 \times \sqrt{0.001675}$, namely 0.535 and 0.341.

Examination of the 95 per cent confidence limits shows they do not overlap, so that we would conclude (other things being equal) that subjects falling in the range (0·535 to 0·341) are normal as regards saliva weight, while subjects with weights of 0·268 or less may well be depressives. A clear-cut distinction between two groups such as has just been demonstrated, is rare in experimental work. In the present example it is due to the fact that the variation between different categories of subjects at any given time of day is remarkably small, so that clear-cut differences can be demonstrated even with very small samples.

The t-tests just demonstrated are valid under the assumption that the two sets of scores are drawn from populations in which the variate or variates being measured are normally distributed with *equal* variance. But the tests are known to be robust so that slight departures from ideal conditions will not seriously affect the inferences made.

9 Analysis of Variance

Introduction

The methods of analysis of variance are now so widely used in experimental work that some knowledge of them is desirable. An introduction to them is given in this chapter.

In earlier chapters we have frequently been concerned with the sum of squares of the deviations of a sample of scores from their mean. It has been written in the form

$$\sum x_i^2 = \sum_{i=1}^{N} (X_i - \overline{X})^2, \qquad\qquad 9.1$$

where the ith score is denoted by X_i and its deviation from the mean, $\overline{X}$, of the sample is x_i. It has also been noted that in general the easiest way to perform the calculations is to use the equivalent formula

$$\sum x_i^2 = \sum X_i^2 - \frac{(\sum X_i)^2}{N}, \qquad\qquad 9.2$$

where N is the number of scores in the sample. For example, if we have the following 12 scores ($N = 12$)

6   8   9   5   4   7   2   10   8   5   3   9,

then
$$\sum X = 6+8+9+\ldots = 76,$$
$$\overline{X} = 6{\cdot}333,$$
and
$$\sum X^2 = 6^2+8^2+9^2+\ldots = 554,$$
so that
$$\sum x^2 = 554 - \frac{76^2}{12} = 72{\cdot}667.$$

Suppose now that the 12 scores are divided arbitrarily into two groups, the first seven scores, say, in one group and the last five in another. We may now inquire how the total sum of squares (namely, 72·67) could be derived by considering the two separate groups.

For the first group, namely

6 8 9 5 4 7 2,

$$n_1 = 7, \quad \sum X = 41, \quad \overline{X} = 5\cdot857, \quad \sum X^2 = 275,$$

hence $\sum x_1^2 = 275 - \dfrac{41^2}{7} = 34\cdot857.$

For the second group, namely

10 8 5 3 9,

$$n_2 = 5, \quad \sum X = 35, \quad \overline{X} = 7\cdot000, \quad \sum X^2 = 279,$$

hence $\sum x_2^2 = 279 - \dfrac{35^2}{5} = 34\cdot000.$

Adding $\Sigma\, x_1^2$ and $\Sigma\, x_2^2$ gives $34\cdot857 + 34\cdot000 = 68\cdot857$, which is the amount of the total sum of squares of $72\cdot667$ which can be accounted for by variation within the two separate groups. The remainder, namely $72\cdot667 - 68\cdot857 = 3\cdot810$, must therefore arise from the separation of the original 12 scores into two groups. Indeed it can be obtained from the over-all mean and the two sample means, $\overline{X} = 6\cdot333$, $\overline{X}_1 = 5\cdot857$ and $\overline{X}_2 = 7\cdot000$, respectively, by the formula

$$n_1(\overline{X}_1 - \overline{X})^2 + n_2(\overline{X}^2 - \overline{X})^2, \qquad\qquad 9.3$$

which gives

$$7(5\cdot857 - 6\cdot333)^2 + 5(7\cdot000 - 6\cdot333)^2 = 3\cdot810,$$

as required. An easier way of doing the calculations is to use the three totals 41, 35 and 76, and the number of scores on which each is based, namely 7, 5 and 12 respectively, in which case we have

$$\frac{41^2}{7} + \frac{35^2}{5} - \frac{76^2}{12} = 3\cdot810.$$

This procedure of partitioning the over-all sum of squares of a set of scores into two parts, one due to variation within subgroups and the other due to variation of the means of the subgroups about the over-all mean, is quite general; it is not confined to a partition into two subgroups only. Moreover, it can be employed when we wish to test for differences between the means of the subgroups themselves. Indeed this is one of the uses implied when the term 'analysis of variance' is used, and we will now see how the procedure works.

Testing the Homogeneity of a Number of Group Means

In Table 6 the scores obtained on a test by four random samples of patients from four different diagnostic categories are given. The sample sizes are respectively $n_1 = 6$, $n_2 = 7$, $n_3 = 5$ and $n_4 = 8$, so that the total number of patients is $N = 26$.

Table 6
Scores for 4 Samples of Patients on a Test

Samples	I	II	III	IV	
	7	4	7	4	
	9	5	5	6	
	10	7	8	3	
	8	4	5	3	
	11	8	6	5	
	9	5		4	
		3		4	
				2	
Sums	54	36	31	31	Total = 152
Means	9·000	5·143	6·200	3·875	Over-all mean = 5·846
Sums of squares	496	204	199	131	Total = 1030
Range	4	5	3	4	

The over-all sum of squares of the deviations of the 26 scores from the general mean 5·846 is (equation **9.2**)

$$\Sigma\, x^2 = 1030 - \frac{152^2}{26} = 141\cdot385.$$

This value must now be partitioned into two parts; one due to variation 'within' the four samples taken separately, and the other due to the variation of the individual sample means about the over-all mean (5·846), or what is generally referred to as variation 'between' samples. The second of these is the easier to find and is as follows:

Sums of squares due to differences between the four sample

$$\text{means} = \frac{54^2}{6} + \frac{36^2}{7} + \frac{31^2}{5} + \frac{31^2}{8} - \frac{152^2}{26}$$

$$= 94·853.$$

Hence, by subtraction, the sums of squares due to variation within the individual samples are

$$141·385 - 94·853 = 46·532.$$

The latter calculation can be checked by finding the sums of squares of the individual samples separately and adding them. We have (using equation **9.2**)

Sample I $\qquad 496 - \dfrac{54^2}{6} = 10·000$

Sample II $\qquad 204 - \dfrac{36^2}{7} = 18·857$

Sample III $\qquad 199 - \dfrac{31^2}{5} = 6·800$

Sample IV $\qquad 131 - \dfrac{31^2}{8} = 10·875$

Total $\qquad\qquad 46·532$

as required.

Having partitioned the over-all sum of squares, the results rounded to the first decimal may now be set out as in Table 7.

Table 7
Analysis of Variance

1 Source of variation	2 d.f.	3 Sums of squares	4 Variance estimate	5 Variance ratio
Between samples	3	94·9	31·63 (s_1^2)	14·96
Within samples	22	46·5	2·11 (s_2^2)	
Total	25	141·4		

In the table the sums of squares are shown in column 3. The degrees of freedom on which each sum of squares is based appear in column 2. Since $N = 26$ the degrees of freedom for the 'total' is $N-1 = 25$. The degrees of freedom for each of the groups separately is n_i-1 and these when added for the four groups give $5+6+4+7 = 22$, which is the number of degrees of freedom for 'within' samples. The remaining degrees of freedom $(25-22)$ are those 'between' samples. Put differently, if there are k samples the degrees of freedom 'between' samples is $k-1$, for if the k means are compared two at a time there are only $k-1$ independent comparisons.

The entries in column 4 of the table, called 'variance estimates', are obtained by dividing the sums of squares in column 3 by their corresponding degrees of freedom, so that 31·63 is 94·9/3 and 2·11 is 46·5/22. An understanding of *analysis of variance* depends largely on getting a clear idea of what these 'variance estimates' represent. Let us look at the value 2·11 which in the table has been labelled s_2^2. Since the sum of squares (46·5) was obtained by finding a sum of squares separately for each sample about its own mean, and afterwards adding them, s_2^2 is an unbiased pooled estimate of the variance of the scores of the four samples of patients. By taking the samples separately the estimate s_2^2 is unaffected by the possibility that the sample means may be very different from each other. This too is why an estimate of over-all variation was not obtained for the 'total' row of the table, for such an estimate could not be relied upon to give an unbiased estimate of variance of patients' scores if the means of the samples themselves differ considerably. In passing, it should also be noted that in estimating s_2^2 certain assumptions are made. The first is that the samples are drawn randomly from populations in which the variable being measured is normally distributed. The second is that the variable has the same variance in each population. Examination of the ranges of the scores for each sample, given in Table 6, suggests that for our data this assumption is met.

Now turn to the estimate of variance 'between' samples, namely 31·63 (labelled s_1^2), in Table 7. It is more difficult to explain, but a simplified explanation is as follows. If the samples are drawn from populations all having the same mean for the variable in question, then it would be reasonable to expect the estimate of variance, s_1^2, simply to reflect variation due to random sampling, and so not to differ from s_2^2. On the other hand if the means of the populations do differ, s_1^2 will reflect this difference, since it is derived from the sample means, and will in general be greater than s_2^2. To test whether s_1^2 is greater than s_2^2 over and above chance fluctuation, we calculate the ratio (called the F-ratio)

$$F = \frac{s_1^2}{s_2^2},$$

which, for the data in Table 7 is 14·96, and refer it to tables of the F-distribution. The latter are given in Appendix 4 for the 5 per cent level of significance and in Appendix 5 for the 1 per cent level of significance. To use the tables we require the degree of freedom on which s_1^2 and s_2^2 respectively are based. They are 3 and 22 respectively (Table 7). Referring to Appendix 4 we find the F-value in column 3, row 22 to be 3·05. Since our value of 14·96 is much greater than this we conclude that s_1^2 is significantly greater than s_2^2 at the 5 per cent level. Referring to Appendix 5 we find the F-value to be 4·82, so that our value is significant beyond the 1 per cent level. We may thus safely conclude that s_1^2 is greater than s_2^2, or that the means of the samples do differ from each other.

Comparing Pairs and Subgroups of Means

The F-ratio test has indicated that the four means in Table 6 are not homogeneous. This does not imply that each differs from every other, so naturally one would want to inquire where the real differences lie. One way of doing this is to compare the means in pairs using t-tests, though such tests tend to exaggerate the significance of differences for means far apart. The tests can be performed readily by using the estimate of variance $s_2^2 = 2 \cdot 11$ from Table 7. For instance if we wish to compare the means for samples II and IV, Table 6, the t-test is

$$t = \frac{5 \cdot 143 - 3 \cdot 875}{\sqrt{\{2 \cdot 11 \, (\frac{1}{7} + \frac{1}{8})\}}},$$
$$= 1 \cdot 69.$$

This value is now referred to the t-distribution (Appendix 2) with 22 degrees of freedom, since the 'within samples' estimate of variance, namely $2 \cdot 11$, is based on this number. The value is found not to reach a reasonable level of significance, hence there is insufficient evidence to claim that the mean scores for populations II and IV differ. In a similar manner each pair of means can be compared.

On the other hand if we wish to compare the average score of a number of samples with that of a number of other samples, it is simpler to work with the sample totals and find an appropriate 'between samples' sum of squares for the comparison required. Suppose we wish to compare the mean for samples II, III and IV, Table 6, with that for sample I. The totals now are

54 and $36 + 31 + 31 = 98$,

based on 6 and 20 scores respectively. The 'between samples' sum of square now is

$$\frac{52^2}{6} + \frac{98^2}{20} - \frac{152^2}{26} = 77 \cdot 6.$$

This is based on 1 degree of freedom since only two totals are being compared, hence the 'between samples' estimate of variance also is $77 \cdot 6$. This can now be compared with the 'within samples' estimate of variance of $2 \cdot 11$ (Table 7). The F-ratio is $77 \cdot 6 / 2 \cdot 11$ which with 1 and 22 degrees of freedom is highly significant. Hence the mean, 9·000, of sample I is seen to differ from the mean for samples II + III + IV, namely $98/20 = 4·9$.

The analysis illustrated in this chapter is known as a one-way analysis of variance. But the method of partitioning an over-all sum of squares into parts, which it illustrates, is very general and can be applied in the analysis of much more complicated problems than that described above.

10 Recording Data on Punch Cards

Introduction

Frequently in observational studies the information required is obtained by asking subjects to fill in answers to questions on a questionnaire, or – if the subjects are interviewed individually – the interviewer may record the answers for them. To facilitate the analysis of the data it is important that the questionnaires be drawn up with care. This is especially so when it is intended to transfer the data on to punch cards for mechanical sorting on a counter-sorting machine, or for analysis by means of an electronic computer.

The standard punch card is rectangular in shape with 80 columns, each containing ten cells numbered 0 to 9. When information from a questionnaire is to be punched on a card, each question or variable is allocated to a column (or adjacent columns) on the card and each of the several possible answers (which should be decided upon in advance) to that question is assigned to a specific cell in the column. The procedure is illustrated by reference to the Item Sheet of the Maudsley–Bethlem Hospitals on which information about the case history, symptomatology, etc., of each in-patient is filled in by the registrar in charge of the case and this information is later punched on cards.

The first piece of information recorded is the patient's hospital number which serves to identify the patient. It is a six-digit number and the first six columns of the card are allocated to it. For example if the number is 246075 then cell 2 is punched in the first column, cell 4 in the second, cell 6 in the third, and so on. For a straightforward variable such as this no difficulties arise.

Since all the information for a single patient cannot be fitted onto the 80 columns of a single card and three cards are required, column 7 of each card is reserved for the 'card number' and has cell '1' punched if the card in question is the first card, cell 2 if it is the second card, etc.

Next we come to the patient's age. On the assumption that no patient will be older than 99 years, only two columns of the card, namely columns 8 and 9 are allocated to age. Hence a patient aged 30 would have cell 3 punched in column 8 and cell 0 punched in column 9. If the patient were aged 7 then we would punch 0 in column 8 and 7 in column 9, though in this case punching the 0 is optional. Of course, if we did not require to record age as accurately as to the nearest year, we could use an interval scale such as the following:

Age in intervals of 10 years

Age	Up to 10	10–19	20–29	30–39	40–49	50–59	60–69	70–79	80+
Cell	0	1	2	3	4	5	6	7	8

and so record the appropriate 10-year interval on a single column, hence saving card space.

Next we come to the patient's sex. It can be recorded on a single column of the card by punching 0 for females and 1 for males, or vice versa. However, where electronic computers are concerned it is generally well to avoid 0 in this context, as most computers read this symbol as a *blank* so that, when we come to check the cards for mispunching, a card from which sex erroneously has been omitted would be counted as though it represented a female. To avoid this possibility we could punch 1 for females and 2 for males. This rule can be followed with advantage in the case of all two-category variables.

It is also important when transferring data onto cards to make provision for 'missing information' and to indicate when an item is 'inapplicable' for a particular subject. These types of information are best allocated to cells at the bottom of a column. For instance if the categories 'not known' and 'not applicable' are allocated to the cells 8 and 9 in a column, then a single instruction in a computer programme, such as 'ignore numbers greater than 7', automatically causes these two categories to be omitted, while an instruction 'ignore numbers greater than 8' causes the 'not applicable' cases to be omitted. Where numerical variables are concerned individuals for whom the information is missing can also be picked up by using some particular coding device. For instance if I.Q., for which scores generally range from about 60 to 140, is allocated three columns on a card then a number outside the possible range, such as 999, could be punched to indicate 'information not available'.

Trivial though these simple rules may at first appear, their observance greatly facilitates the analysis of data recorded on cards. To achieve this advantage to the full a questionnaire must be designed to comply with the rules. Frequently it is helpful to classify the questions or variables in advance. Three useful and commonly occurring classes are the following:

1. *Numerical variables* such as age, I.Q., etc.
2. *Binary variables*   such as sex, or variables with answers such as 'yes – no', 'right – wrong', etc.
3. *Polylog variables*   such as the age distribution given on page 112 or semantic scales. For example a subject may be rated on a variable such as *outcome* according to the scale – 'recovered, improved, no change, slightly worse, much worse'.

Numerical variables generally require two, three or more adjacent columns on a card, while binary and polylog variables usually can be accommodated on a single column.

But these three types of item are not necessarily mutually exclusive. Suppose, for example, we wish to get information about the age of a patient's mother at the time that he was born. The question might then be a direct one to this effect providing an answer in the form of a numerical variable. But many patients might have difficulty in supplying the information exactly. In view of this a polylog-type variable might be more reasonable and we could ask the patient to circle one of the following age ranges instead:

At the time of your birth your mother's age was –
1. Under 20 years,   4. 40 years or over,
2. 20–29 years,   8. not known.
3. 30–39 years,

It is advisable too when designing a questionnaire to avoid open-ended questions. For instance if a patient is asked a question such as the following – 'With whom do you intend to live when you leave hospital?', a variety of answers must be expected and much effort will be needed in classifying them before the information can be usefully employed. But if the question is carefully formulated in advance, and clarity achieved about the type of information that would be useful, confusion can be avoided. A possible formulation of the question might be as follows:

Discharge living arrangements
1. With your spouse or parents,
2. cohabiting,
3. with other relatives or friends,
4. living alone,
5. other arrangements,
8. not known,
9. not applicable.

Polylog questions too can often be designed to record in a straightforward way information for a variable for which there are several possibilities. For example, information commonly required about a patient's twin, if he has one, might be fitted on a single column of a card as follows –

Twin
1. No,
2. yes, alive, same sex,
3. yes, alive, opposite sex,
4. yes, dead, same sex,
5. yes, dead, opposite sex,
6. yes, dead, sex not known,
7. yes, sex known but not known whether alive or dead,
8. yes, sex not known, and not known whether alive or dead,
9. not known whether twin.

Errors in Card Punching

Due to the human element it is normal to expect a small percentage of errors when data are punched on cards. For this reason it is always wise to have the punching verified and this process is facilitated if a card verifier, in addition to a card-punching machine, is available. But errors in punching can be greatly reduced if the questionnaire is laid out in a manner convenient for the punch-machine operator. For this reason it is now customary to enter beside each item or question in a questionnaire the column number, or numbers, allotted to the question on the card, as well as the cell numbers in which the different categories of answer are to be punched. Here is an example from the Hospital Item Sheet referred to earlier.

		Yes	*No*	*N.A.*
Job obtained at discharge	79	1	2	9

The number *79* refers to the column on the card allocated to the item, while the numbers in the boxes refer to the cells in the column in which the different responses are to be punched (N.A. = not applicable, and would refer for instance to a child, or to a housewife). If there is more than one card per person, this information too could be indicated: for instance we might print 79:1 for column 79 on the first card, 35:2 for column 35 on the second card, and so on.

Facilitating Cross-Tabulation

When the data are to be analysed on an electronic computer, it matters little if more than one card per subject is required, for the computer programme can be written to collate data from one card with another. But if the sorting of the cards is to be done mechanically on a counter-sorter, it greatly facilitates matters if variables for which cross-tabulations are likely to be required appear on the same card. For the Hospital Item Sheet this end was achieved in part by punching some essential core data – for instance, the patient's age, sex, diagnosis, marital status, treatment, duration of stay, outcome, etc. – on each card used.

It is generally essential, and especially so if mathematical operations are to be performed on the data, that single punching only is used. In other words the design of a questionnaire should be such that a card never has more than a single cell punched on each column. This requirement refers, of course, only to variables; when a computer programme is punched on cards, and symbols other than digits are involved, multiple punching is used intentionally to indicate letters and symbols other than numerals.

The Use of Computers

Electronic computers are now extensively used by research workers for the analysis of data which arise in field investigations and controlled laboratory experiments. This is especially the case when the sample of subjects involved is large and several variables are being considered simultaneously. Access to computers is now relatively easy and programs exist for most of the more common types of analyses required. Yet the research worker should remember that a computer is not essential for research and many of the simple statistical methods described in this book can be carried out quite easily on a pocket calculator or simple desk machine.

Appendix 1

The Normal Distribution Function*

Fractional area under the normal probability curve between the mean and the given ordinates (checked against Pearson's Table 2).

A decimal point should precede each number in the body of the table.

z	0·00	0·01	0·02	0·03	0·04	0·05	0·06	0·07	0·08	0·09
0·0	5000	5040	5080	5120	5160	5199	5239	5279	5319	5359
0·1	5398	5438	5478	5517	5557	5596	5636	5675	5714	5753
0·2	5793	5832	5871	5910	5984	5987	6026	6064	6103	6141
0·3	6179	6217	6255	6293	6331	6368	6406	6443	6480	6517
0·4	6554	6591	6628	6664	6700	6736	6772	6808	6844	6879
0·5	6915	6950	6985	7019	7054	7088	7123	7157	7190	7224
0·6	7257	7291	7324	7357	7389	7422	7454	7486	7517	7549
0·7	7580	7611	7642	7673	7704	7734	7764	7794	7823	7852
0·8	7881	7910	7939	7967	7995	8023	8051	8078	8106	8133
0·9	8159	8186	8212	8238	8264	8289	8315	8340	8365	8389
1·0	8413	8438	8461	8485	8508	8531	8554	8577	8599	8621
1·1	8643	8665	8686	8708	8729	8749	8770	8790	8810	8830
1·2	8849	8869	8888	8907	8925	8944	8962	8980	8997	9015
1·3	9032	9049	9066	9082	9099	9115	9131	9147	9162	9177
1·4	9192	9207	9222	9236	9251	9265	9279	9292	9306	9319
1·5	9332	9345	9357	9370	9382	9394	9406	9418	9429	9441
1·6	9452	9463	9474	9484	9495	9505	9515	9525	9535	9545
1·7	9554	9564	9573	9582	9591	9599	9608	9616	9625	9633
1·8	9641	9649	9656	9664	9671	9678	9686	9693	9699	9706
1·9	9713	9719	9726	9732	9738	9744	9750	9756	9761	9767
2·0	97725	97778	97831	97882	97932	97982	98030	98077	98124	98169
2·1	98214	98257	98300	98341	98382	98422	98461	98500	98537	98574
2·2	98610	98645	98679	98713	98745	98778	98809	98840	98870	98899
2·3	98928	98956	98983	99010	99036	99061	99086	99111	99134	99158
2·4	99180	99202	99224	99245	99266	99286	99305	99324	99343	99361
2·5	99379	99396	99413	99430	99446	99461	99477	99492	99506	99520
2·6	99534	99547	99560	99573	99585	99598	99609	99621	99632	99643
2·7	99653	99664	99674	99683	99693	99702	99711	99720	99728	99736
2·8	99744	99752	99760	99767	99774	99781	99788	99795	99801	99807
2·9	99813	99819	99825	99831	99836	99841	99846	99851	99856	99861

*K. Pearson, *Tables for Statisticians and Biometricians, Part 1* (3rd edn), Biometrika Office, University College, London, 1942.

Appendix 2

The *t*-Distribution*

d.f.	P=0·1	0·05	0·02	0·01	0·001
1	6·314	12·706	31·821	63·657	636·619
2	2·920	4·303	6·965	9·925	31·598
3	2·353	3·182	4·541	5·841	12·924
4	2·132	2·776	3·747	4·604	8·610
5	2·015	2·571	3·365	4·032	6·859
6	1·943	2·447	3·143	3·707	5·959
7	1·895	2·365	2·998	3·499	5·408
8	1·860	2·306	2·896	3·355	5·041
9	1·833	2·262	2·821	3·250	4·781
10	1·812	2·228	2·764	3·169	4·587
11	1·796	2·201	2·718	3·106	4·437
12	1·782	2·179	2·681	3·055	4·318
13	1·771	2·160	2·650	3·012	4·221
14	1·761	2·145	2·624	2·977	4·140
15	1·753	2·131	2·602	2·947	4·073
16	1·746	2·120	2·583	2·921	4·015
17	1·740	2·110	2·567	2·898	3·965
18	1·734	2·101	2·552	2·878	3·922
19	1·729	2·093	2·539	2·861	3·883
20	1·725	2·086	2·528	2·845	3·850
21	1·721	2·080	2·518	2·831	3·819
22	1·717	2·074	2·508	2·819	3·792
23	1·714	2·069	2·500	2·807	3·767
24	1·711	2·064	2·492	2·797	3·745
25	1·708	2·060	2·485	2·787	3·725
26	1·706	2·056	2·479	2·779	3·707
27	1·703	2·052	2·473	2·771	3·690
28	1·701	2·048	2·467	2·763	3·674
29	1·699	2·045	2·462	2·756	3·659
30	1·697	2·042	2·457	2·750	3·646
40	1·684	2·021	2·423	2·704	3·551
60	1·671	2·000	2·390	2·660	3·460
120	1·658	1·980	2·358	2·617	3·373
∞	1·645	1·960	2·326	2·576	3·291

* Abridged from Table 3 of Fisher and Yates, *Statistical Tables for Biological, Agricultural and Medical Research*, Oliver & Boyd, Edinburgh, by permission of the publishers.

Appendix 3

Percentage Points of the χ^2 Distribution*

d.f.	$P=0.050$	0.025	0.010	0.001
1	3·841	5·024	6·635	10·828
2	5·991	7·378	9·210	13·816
3	7·815	9·348	11·345	16·266
4	9·488	11·143	13·277	18·467
5	11·071	21·833	15·086	20·515
6	12·592	14·449	16·812	22·458
7	14·067	16·013	18·475	24·322
8	15·507	17·535	20·090	26·125
9	16·919	19·023	21·666	27·877
10	18·307	20·483	23·209	29·588
11	19·675	21·920	24·725	31·264
12	21·026	23·337	26·217	32·909
13	22·362	24·736	27·688	34·528
14	23·685	26·119	29·141	36·123
15	24·996	27·488	30·578	37·697
16	26·296	28·845	32·000	39·252
17	27·587	30·191	33·409	40·790
18	28·869	31·526	34·805	42·312
19	30·144	32·852	36·191	43·820
20	31·410	34·170	37·566	45·315
21	32·671	35·479	38·932	46·797
22	33·924	36·781	40·289	48·268
23	35·173	38·076	41·638	49·728
24	36·415	39·364	42·980	51·179
25	37·653	40·647	44·314	52·620
26	38·885	41·923	45·642	54·052
27	40·113	43·194	46·963	55·476
28	41·337	44·461	48·278	56·892
29	42·557	45·722	49·588	58·302
30	43·773	46·979	50·892	59·703
40	55·759	59·342	63·691	73·402
50	67·505	71·420	76·154	86·661
60	79·082	83·298	88·379	99·607
80	101·879	106·629	112·329	124·839
100	124·342	129·561	135·807	149·449

*Abridged from Table 8 of E. S. Pearson and H. O. Hartley, *Biometrika Tables for Statisticians* vol. 1, Cambridge University Press, 1954, by permission of Professor E. S. Pearson on behalf of the Biometrika Trustees.

Appendix 4

The Variance Ratio (F) 5 Per Cent Points*
$(P = 0.05)$

n_1 n_2	1	2	3	4	5	6	8	12	24	∞
3	10·13	9·55	9·28	9·12	9·01	8·94	8·84	8·74	8·64	8·53
4	7·71	6·94	6·59	6·39	6·26	6·16	6·04	5·91	5·77	5·63
5	6·61	5·79	5·41	5·19	5·05	4·95	4·82	4·68	4·53	4·36
6	5·99	5·14	4·76	4·53	4·39	4·28	4·15	4·00	3·84	3·67
7	5·59	4·74	4·35	4·12	3·97	3·87	3·73	3·57	3·41	3·23
8	5·32	4·46	4·07	3·84	3·69	3·58	3·44	3·28	3·12	2·93
9	5·12	4·26	3·86	3·63	3·48	3·37	3·23	3·07	2·90	2·71
10	4·96	4·10	3·71	3·48	3·33	3·22	3·07	2·91	2·74	2·54
11	4·84	3·98	3·59	3·36	3·20	3·09	2·95	2·79	2·61	2·40
12	4·75	3·88	3·49	3·26	3·11	3·00	2·85	2·69	2·50	2·30
13	4·67	3·80	3·41	3·18	3·02	2·92	2·77	2·60	2·42	2·21
14	4·60	3·74	3·34	3·11	2·96	2·85	2·70	2·53	2·35	2·13
15	4·54	3·68	3·29	3·06	2·90	2·79	2·64	2·48	2·29	2·07
16	4·49	3·63	3·24	3·01	2·85	2·74	2·59	2·42	2·24	2·01
17	4·45	3·59	3·20	2·96	2·81	2·70	2·55	2·38	2·19	1·96
18	4·41	3·55	3·16	2·93	2·77	2·66	2·51	2·34	2·15	1·92
19	4·38	3·52	3·13	2·90	2·74	2·63	2·48	2·31	2·11	1·88
20	4·35	3·49	3·10	2·87	2·71	2·60	2·45	2·28	2·08	1·84
21	4·32	3·47	3·07	2·84	2·68	2·57	2·42	2·25	2·05	1·81
22	4·30	3·44	3·05	2·82	2·66	2·55	2·40	2·23	2·03	1·78
23	4·28	3·42	3·03	2·80	2·64	2·53	2·38	2·20	2·00	1·76
24	4·26	3·40	3·01	2·78	2·62	2·51	2·36	2·18	1·98	1·73
25	4·24	3·38	2·99	2·76	2·60	2·49	2·34	2·16	1·96	1·71
26	4·22	3·37	2·98	2·74	2·59	2·47	2·32	2·15	1·95	1·69
27	4·21	3·35	2·96	2·73	2·57	2·46	2·30	2·13	1·93	1·67
28	4·20	3·34	2·95	2·71	2·56	2·44	2·29	2·12	1·91	1·65
29	4·18	3·33	2·93	2·70	2·54	2·43	2·28	2·10	1·90	1·64
30	4·17	3·32	2·92	2·69	2·53	2·42	2·27	2·09	1·89	1·62
40	4·08	3·23	2·84	2·61	2·45	2·34	2·18	2·00	1·79	1·51
60	4·00	3·15	2·76	2·52	2·37	2·25	2·10	1·92	1·70	1·39
120	3·92	3·07	2·68	2·45	2·29	2·17	2·02	1·83	1·61	1·25
∞	3·84	2·99	2·60	2·37	2·21	2·10	1·94	1·75	1·52	1·00

* Abridged from Table 5 of Fisher and Yates, *Statistical Tables for Biological, Agricultural and Medical Research*, Oliver & Boyd, Edinburgh, by permission of the publishers.

Appendix 5

The Variance Ratio (F) 1 Per Cent Points
($P = 0.01$)

n_1 n_2	1	2	3	4	5	6	8	12	24	∞
3	34·12	30·82	29·46	28·71	28·24	27·91	27·49	27·05	26·60	26·12
4	21·20	18·00	16·69	15·98	15·52	15·21	14·80	14·37	13·93	13·46
5	16·26	13·27	12·06	11·39	10·97	10·67	10·29	9·89	9·47	9·02
6	13·74	10·92	9·78	9·15	8·75	8·47	8·10	7·72	7·31	6·88
7	12·25	9·55	8·45	7·85	7·46	7·19	6·84	6·47	6·07	5·65
8	11·26	8·65	7·59	7·01	6·63	6·37	6·03	5·67	5·28	4·86
9	10·56	8·02	6·99	6·42	6·06	5·80	5·47	5·11	4·73	4·31
10	10·04	7·56	6·55	5·99	5·64	5·39	5·06	4·71	4·33	3·91
11	9·65	7·20	6·22	5·67	5·32	5·07	4·74	4·40	4·02	3·60
12	9·33	6·93	5·95	5·41	5·06	4·82	4·50	4·16	3·78	3·36
13	9·07	6·70	5·74	5·20	4·86	4·62	4·30	3·96	3·59	3·16
14	8·86	6·51	5·56	5·03	4·69	4·46	4·14	3·80	3·43	3·00
15	8·68	6·36	5·42	4·89	4·56	4·32	4·00	3·67	3·29	2·87
16	8·53	6·23	5·29	4·77	4·44	4·20	3·89	3·55	3·18	2·75
17	8·40	6·11	5·18	4·67	4·34	4·10	3·79	3·45	3·08	2·65
18	8·28	6·01	5·09	4·58	4·25	4·01	3·71	3·37	3·00	2·57
19	8·18	5·93	5·01	4·50	4·17	3·94	3·63	3·30	2·92	2·49
20	8·10	5·85	4·94	4·43	4·10	3·87	3·56	3·23	2·86	2·42
21	8·02	5·78	4·87	4·37	4·04	3·81	3·51	3·17	2·80	2·36
22	7·94	5·72	4·82	4·31	3·99	3·76	3·45	3·12	2·75	2·31
23	7·88	5·66	4·76	4·26	3·94	3·71	3·41	3·07	2·70	2·26
24	7·82	5·61	4·72	4·22	3·90	3·67	3·36	3·03	2·66	2·21
25	7·77	5·57	4·68	4·18	3·86	3·63	3·32	2·99	2·62	2·17
26	7·72	5·53	4·64	4·14	3·82	3·59	3·29	2·96	2·58	2·13
27	7·68	5·49	4·60	4·11	3·78	3·56	3·26	2·93	2·55	2·10
28	7·64	5·45	4·57	4·07	3·75	3·53	3·23	2·90	2·52	2·06
29	7·60	5·42	4·54	4·04	3·73	3·50	3·20	2·87	2·49	2·03
30	7·56	5·39	4·51	4·02	3·70	3·47	3·17	2·84	2·47	2·01
40	7·31	5·18	4·31	3·83	3·51	3·29	2·99	2·66	2·29	1·80
60	7·08	4·98	4·13	3·65	3·34	3·12	2·82	2·50	2·12	1·60
120	6·85	4·79	3·95	3·48	3·17	2·96	2·66	2·34	1·95	1·38
∞	6·64	4·60	3·78	3·32	3·02	2·80	2·51	2·18	1·79	1·00

* Abridged from Table 5 of Fisher and Yates, *Statistical Tables for Biological, Agricultural and Medical Research*, Oliver & Boyd, Edinburgh, by permission of the publishers.

References

ARTHURS, A. M. (1965), *Probability Theory*, Routledge & Kegan Paul.

COX, D. R. (1958), *Planning of Experiments*, Wiley.

DAVIES, D. L., and STEIN, L. (1963), 'What becomes of Maudsley Registrars?', *Proc. Roy. Soc. Med.*, vol. 56, pp. 115–19.

EVERITT, B. S. (1968), 'Moments of the statistics Kappa and Weighted Kappa', *Brit. J. math. stat. Psychol.*, vol. 21, pp. 97–103.

FINNEY, D. J. (1963), *Tables for Testing Significance in 2 × 2 Contingency Tables*, Cambridge University Press.

FISHER, R. A., and YATES, F. (1963), *Statistical Tables for Biological, Agricultural and Medical Research*, Oliver & Boyd.

FLETCHER, C. M. (1960), 'Criteria for diagnosis and assessment in clinical trials', in Hill, A. B. (ed.), *Controlled Clinical Trials*, Blackwell.

FOULDS, G. A. (1963), 'The design of experiments in psychiatry', in Sainsbury, P., and Kreitman, N. (eds.), *Methods of Psychiatric Research*, Oxford University Press.

HAMILTON, M. (1959), 'The assessment of anxiety states by rating', *Brit. J. med. Psychol.*, vol. 32, pp. 50–55.

HILL, A. B. (1960), *Controlled Clinical Trials*, Blackwell.

HINTON, J. M. (1961), 'The actions of amylobarbitone sodium, butobarbitone and quinalbarbitone sodium upon insomnia and nocturnal restlessness compared in psychiatric patients', *Brit. J. Pharmacol.*, vol. 16, pp. 82–9.

HUITSON, A. (1966), *The Analysis of Variance*, Charles Griffin.

KALTON, G. (1966), *Introduction to Statistical Ideas for Social Scientists*, Chapman & Hall.

KNOWLES, J. B. (1963), 'Rating methods and measurement of behaviour', in Sainsbury, P., and Kreitman, N. (eds.), *Methods of Psychiatric Research*, Oxford University Press.

LORD, F. M., and NOVICK, M. R. (1968), *Statistical Theories of Mental Test Scores*, Addison–Wesley, pp. 105–16.

MAXWELL, A. E. (1961), *Analysing Qualitative Data*, Methuen.

MAXWELL, A. E., and PILLINER, A. E. G. (1968), 'Deriving coefficients of reliability and agreement between raters', *Brit. J. math. stat. Psychol.*, vol. 21, pp. 105–16.

McNEMAR, Q. (1962), *Psychological Statistics*, 3rd edn, Wiley.

MOSER, C. A. (1958), *Survey Methods in Social Investigation*, Heinemann.

MOSTELLER, F., ROURKE, R. E. K., and THOMAS, G. B. (1962), *Probability with Statistical Applications*, Addison-Wesley.

PASAMANICK, B., ROGERS, M. E., and LILIENFELD, A. M. (1956), 'Pregnancy experience and the development of behavior disorder in children', *Am. J. Psychiat.*, vol. 112, pp. 613–51.

REID, D. D. (1954), 'The design of clinical experiments', *Lancet*, vol. 2, pp. 1293–5.

SAINSBURY, P., and KREITMAN, N. (1963), *Methods of Psychiatric Research*, Oxford University Press.

SCOTT, J. A. (1962), 'Intelligence, physique and family size', *Brit. J. prev. soc. Med.*, vol. 16, pp. 165–73.

SHAPIRO, M. B. (1963), 'A clinical approach to fundamental research with special reference to the study of the single patient', in Sainsbury, P., and Kreitman, N. (eds.), *Methods of Psychiatric Research*, Oxford University Press.

YEOMANS, K. A. (1968), *Statistics for the Social Scientist*, vol. 1: *Introducing Statistics*, Penguin.

Index